FOOD MEMORIES

REAGAN LAKINS

(Eventually Known As)

raVen

Copyright 2020 Reagan Lakins

All rights reserved. No part of this book may be reproduced, stored in a retrieval system or transmitted, in any form or by any means, without the prior written consent of the publisher.

Disclaimer: This is a work of memory, not historical fact. All names beyond my own have been changed to honor the privacy of those involved in my story.

Editing by Zoe Quinton

Cover design by Reagan "raVen" Lakins and Karen Ronan

Interior design by Reagan "raVen" Lakins, Karen Ronan and Wendy Craig

Acknowledgments

To the first peoples of Switzerland, who were colonized
To the first peoples of Germany, who were colonized
To the first peoples of Scandinavia, who were colonized
To the first peoples of Lithuania, who were colonized
To the first peoples of the Netherlands, who were colonized
To the first peoples of British Isles, who were colonized
To the first peoples of the Americas, who were colonized
To the first peoples of The Great Utah Basin, who were colonized
To the first peoples of the West Coast of the Americas, where I now stand, who were colonized

To the first plant, animal and living beings, who were colonized
To the meat, vegetable, herb, tree, crops, who were colonized
To the plots of land that will never see the sun under concrete, colonized
To the trauma, disconnection and forgetting that lives on in my bones, blood and gut, colonized

To the sicknesses that are trying to help me see

May I find a way to understand
May I find a way to respect
May I find a way to honor
May I find a way to clear
May I find a way to remember

These hands
These white hands, open
These blue eyes, open
This raw, beating heart, open
Aching

To all who have been a part of me
To all who have suffered
And to all I am a part of
May we find a way
To remember
Our privilege
This privilege
This Body
This Earth
May we find a way

And to Pamela and the Sisters of the Holy Pen, I love you.

Food Memories

FORWARD

This book almost didn't get published.

The process of writing down these memories was freeing, creative, enjoyable. Watching what images wanted to be included was somewhat like a mystery I would sit down to discover each time I opened my blank document. More and more showed up, and many months went by of me being totally swept away by the re-telling of these stories through my fingers. Yet poised at the final edge of the process, I thought, or rather something thought, that this was a totally insane thing to do.

Not the writing of it all—I'd been doing this for years in secret journals. But the revealing of these guts to you! How you saw me before this offering, the image of mystery or toughness or wisdom (or whatever...who knows) you've held—that all of this would be challenged by sharing this with the world. All the embarrassing moments, the exposure of what I do behind closed doors, the shame, the hiding I've done over the years, all tugging at me to keep this collection of memories from your eyes. What would happen if I let you see me like this? What terrible things would happen? And what if nothing happened? What if you didn't care, if what I thought of as my helpful description of my "dark night of the soul" did not in some way have meaning for you? What if my writing wasn't sophisticated enough, or not the quality of what you thought I might produce? What if my journey, my words, somehow *hurt* you? Why expose myself at the risk of these possibilities? Why?

Since you have this book in your hot little hands, it is obvious I didn't let that voice hold me back. I did the crazy thing and let these words, these approximations of my character, these windows into what most people would never admit to, I let them out into the world.

The simple image of you, holding this book, possibly feeling comforted, not alone, and somewhat understood is what kept me going. I hope in some way it reaches this goal.

Ps. As you head into reading, know that part of the nature of my narrative holds periods without clarity or a linear evolution and that this is reflected in the prose. I have used poems and brief statements to attempt to somewhat keep the thread from breaking. I have placed the symbol of a labyrinth, the ancient structural metaphor for the seemingly confusing twists and turns of life at the tops of these descriptions.

However, it was my intention that my readers contemplate the fuzziness of parts of the book as being reflective of the fuzziness of my mind during the experience of the eating disorder and life challenges I went through as a result. If you feel confused at any point, if it feels like you're too lost to go on, just remember the symbol of a labyrinth. Remember the spiral nature, of the in- and-out of seasons, and trust that you'll get to the center if you just keep going.

Thanks for walking with me.

~raVen

PART ONE

In the beginning, she felt free and playful when she ate.

In the beginning, there was the forest, fantasy creatures and mysteries to be solved. Food was one of her favorite pleasures, but it was not the only thing. Her body was a vehicle for many joyous things, and not something to fear or be confused by.

In the beginning, she felt free and playful when she ate and couldn't understand why her mother never did.

1

Vanilla Ice Cream

1982. Eight years old.

I am sitting in the living room of the apartment on Taylor Street.

The couch is stiff and kinda scratchy against my bare legs—I'm in shorts because it's a warm morning. In my lap rests a gingham-checked towel, and on top of this, a cold bowl of vanilla ice cream. I'm excited to eat it, but am waiting for a few moments until its surface goes from an icy shield to a creamy yielding.

I look up and out our sliding glass windows, where the Monterey pines are subtly swaying in a dense blanket of typical fog and mist. To my right is the TV console. I'm kinda excited because I read that *Beastmaster* is on this early in the morning. It's a typical fantasy movie, where the hero goes on an adventure to rescue a kidnapped maiden, but I like this way of telling it: filled with animal familiars and scary witches and shape-shifting, creepy creatures. I pick up the TV remote and slide my fingers across the buttons until I find the power switch, then press it to get to HBO.

Marc Singer, as Dar the hero, comes onto the screen, trudging through the desert with his trusty black tiger. I swoon to be by his side like Kiri, the abducted but hardy maiden.

But...I want to be Dar the magnificent! Why do I also have this stupid girly desire to be Kiri—saved by him? Gross!

I look down at my bowl and it seems the time is right to pierce the golden goodness with my spoon. I reach over to the coffee table and pick up the spoon, being careful not to tip over the bowl in my moving. I settle back into the couch and prepare to enjoy, lifting the spoon and letting it dive-bomb playfully into the ice cream.

"Kaboom!" I jab the utensil's edges through the resistance, scooping up enough for a bite. "Whirrrrr!" I lift and soar the spoon around and into my mouth, finally closing my lips around its cool perimeter.

I feel the milky denseness collapse slowly against the roof of my mouth. I leave the spoon inside and feel the form become liquid. It streams around the sides of the spoon, travelling down onto my tongue and filling my head with frozen joy. I smile and look back up at the TV, spoon sticking out of my mouth. I see that Kiri and Dar the Beastmaster are playing with Kodo and Podo, his pet ferrets. *Man...I wish I had that life!*

For a moment, I dream of being summoned on an adventure with my telepathically-connected pet tiger and ferrets. I think of what it would be like to merge with my familiar, the Hawk, and to see through its eyes like the Beastmaster does—to feel that connected to the animal world, to be special and chosen for a great mission. *But wait! If the Kingdom of Aruk had ice cream, my mission would be to conquer this bowl of deliciousness and beyond! I...will...conquer!* I switch from a moment of longing to laughing and looking forward to my current edible adventure.

I hold my spoon up high and again send it to dive-bomb into the ice foam. I wind the weighted spoon around in the air, finally placing it inside my mouth to savor once again. The rich ambrosia rests on my tongue, melting. I slide the spoon out of my slightly parted lips and put it down, closing my eyes. Aside from the yowling and battle scene noises coming from the TV, the rest of the house is quiet. I am not alone, but my mother is sleeping.

2

COFFEEMATE

I am sitting on the kitchen counter.

Its ledge is pushing through my pants and into my legs. To my left, the smoke-stained cupboard is wide open, and I can see the Coffeemate sitting there, waiting for me. I pull it down and onto the counter and pick up the spoon resting on the linoleum. I scoop a mound of creamy crystals into my mouth. I can feel this mountain of goodness clumping as it hits the moisture of my saliva, the curious sensation of it suddenly collapsing as I hold it on my tongue, savoring.

I take in a few more spoonfuls and decide I want something salty. I look back into the cupboard to see what awaits me. I see that there are a few cans of Dinty Moore beef stew and decide this will be my next delight. I look outside to my right, out the kitchen window, and notice that the trees have become black silhouettes. I wonder where my mom is, it's getting way later than when she usually comes home from the coffee shop. I decide that Dinty Moore is even more appropriate, as now it seems like it will be my dinner.

I take down Dinty from the cupboard and set it on the counter. I hop off the edge, my feet go *plop!* onto the floor. The key-laden chain around my neck bounces off my shirt and rests again there as I quickly steady myself. I go to the drawer where the can opener is and slide it open. It smells like menthol cigarettes and there are traces of broken potato chips and tobacco scattered beneath various utensils. I ruffle through this, grimacing, and grab the instrument. I shuffle back across the floor to Dinty, place the can opener on the rim and feel the *pop!* of the circular blade as it pokes into the can's surface. I twist the knob on the opener and listen to the *squeak, squeak* on its trip around the edges, until finally the lid caves in.

Gooey brown liquid seeps out from the crevice, and I peel the lid back carefully to reveal the can's full glory. Chunks float on the surface, of white and orange and dark sinew. I pick up the Coffeemate-dusted spoon and dip it into the stew, bringing a towering mass of it to my mouth. As the substance enters, I can feel the saltiness of the potatoes and the soft, golden carrots against the surfaces of my tongue. I remove the spoon and squish the tender objects against the roof of my mouth. The cold congealed fat globules leave a pasty residue behind as I swallow. I close my eyes and enjoy.

I am not thinking of where my mother is now. It's just me and my good pal Dinty.

3

FLIPPING DOGS

It is my birthday.

I am standing a few feet away from the front door, I can feel the plush tendrils of the brown carpet squishing through my toes. Someone has come and is knocking. I am watching my mother standing at the door, cracked open only slightly, as a hushed conversation takes place between them. She opens the door more widely and I see it is him: my father. Somehow I get the sense that my mother and this man have made a tense agreement to let him take me out to dinner for my birthday.

He is coming in the door and I am now being led to his side. I place my small hand in his large, bony, cold fingers. Like I'm supposed to. I know, somehow, that this man is my father, but I don't really know him. My parents have been divorced for many years, and mom rarely lets him see me, or at least that's "the story." On this night, she has for some reason let him in the house. He kneels in front of me, says hello and smiles at me. I feel the warmth in my heart that seems to come from his words.

Cold hands. Warm heart?

We drive to Cannery Row and I get out of the limousine he had come and whisked me away in. I feel like a star. The door opens and the coldness of his large hand envelops tentatively around mine. He pulls, urging me to come out and explore the night air. We walk to the front of a large wooden building, a restaurant that looks as if it could be part of an old pirate or western movie set. Above me, his long arm reaches out to the door and opens it for my tiny body to walk through. He enters behind me and the door whooshes shut.

The sounds and smells are overwhelming, alcohol fuming sailor types are making a ruckus at the bar. I hear clinking of ice in glasses, and dishes being slammed into bus trays. We are led through and past all of this to the back of the restaurant. On our way I reach out to touch the raw and splintering walls and tables, being careful to not get poked. This is all very exciting compared to the sameness of me and mom at Bob's Big Boy, or eating at the living room table, alone.

We get to our reserved spot. My father isn't saying much as I look up at him. He's a million miles tall. One side of the table is a booth-like seat, the other is flanked by chairs. My butt squeaks along the pleather as I situate myself on the booth side. He pulls out a worn chair on the opposite side of the table, it scrapes loudly along the floor with a squealing sound, and he sits down in the seat. We are across from each other, in nervous silence, but he smiles at me. All that matters is that he smiles at me.

At some point he places a stuffed toy dog on the table in front of my tiny folded arms. He reaches under its polyester stomach and switches a lever. I watch as it flips over electronically and yips out loud, annoyingly.

I don't remember what I ate, or what he ate, but we were at the table, together.

4

SOURGRASS

Sunrays warm my eyelids.

I've just woken and have become fascinated by the red-orange-black pulsing patterns behind them. Slowly I peel my eyes open, looking to the stucco ceiling, slightly tanned by my mother's heavy second-hand smoke. I lie there for a moment, rearranging myself. The *squeak squeak* of the daybed beneath me echoes in the quiet of the morning.

My pasty tongue runs over the surfaces of my teeth. I can feel bits of the granola I chomped on a few hours ago when I woke to the early light. After stuffing handfuls of crispy sweetness into my hungry mouth, I got real tired and fell back to sleep. Here I am up again. My belly still feels full, but I'm thirsty.

Jumper runs into the room and pounces promptly on my face. His warm fur partially suffocates me, but not enough so that I can't giggle. I push him aside, roll over and snuggle with him. My ear settles on his stomach and the long, luxurious purrs vibrate my little head. I'm in a cocoon, here with my furry friend, and there is no yelling and screaming.

Now that I'm on my side, I can see out the large window above my bed. A crystal blue sky hovers above the neighbor's tall pine trees, and it seems to be calling to me: *Come out, come out, come out and play.*

Excited, I smooch Jumper on the forehead and whilst spitting out cat hairs throw off my covers. I swing my legs over the edge, stand up and shuffle my way to the closet to get dressed. *What the day has in store, the day's great adventure!*

I tiptoe out my bedroom door, and into the bathroom. I go to the sink and turn the faucet on to a trickle, putting my mouth under the tap and capturing the stream. Cool water flows down over the sides of my cheeks, and into my parched throat. I swallow a few luscious liquidy gulps. I feel the cold metal faucet knob as I turn it off, and the back of my arm slides over my face to wipe the beads of moisture away.

I emerge from the watering station and continue down the short hall past my mother's bedroom. She's still asleep and I'm quiet to make sure it stays that way. I love the silence and space I have when she's not awake. The floorboards creak slightly with my steps through the living room. I'm holding my breath so the sounds won't wake her.

I open the front door, considering it the first leg of my great adventure, the first test passed, not waking the sleeping, dangerous dragon. As I step out into the sun, birdsong greets my ears, and I smile so big. I breathe in the fresh air and instinctively reach for my neck, checking to see if my key chain is there in case she's gone when I return. *Never know where the adventure might take me! Better be sure!*

I make my way down the olive-green staircase, its paint peeling and rough stair grips coming up at the edges. I always want to run my hand down the banister, but know I risk splinters if I do, so instead my hand hovers and glides over it on my way down. I look around me at the bottom of the stairs, listening in to the birds, the wind, seeing if anything interesting grabs my eye. *What do I wanna do today? Hmmm.*

I look down the street and see the house on the corner. The witch's house. I decide to go towards it and see what happens.

I skip across the street at the intersection, and then finally arrive at the old, dilapidated gate that surrounds the witch's house. No one ever seems to be here, but there are so many curious artifacts around it suggests something mysterious lives within. Across the yard, various jewel tones of empty glass bottles line up to cover the insides of the wooden cabin windows. I watch them glisten. Closer to me a great globe shimmers from the center of the wild and unkempt garden. Various feral felines skitter across my line of vision through the greenery. *I wonder what my life would be like if I lived here, with the* old witch. Maybe she would teach me spells and we'd stir potions together. Maybe she'd tell me stories as we sat in front of the hearth each night together. Or maybe, she'd eat me. I wonder if she's a good witch or a bad witch, and who feeds her cats if there's no one home? Maybe she's just a...spirit?

I catch myself in thought and take a breath, looking around and figuring out what to do next. I can't just stand here, my body is tingling with too much energy. It wants to do something more on this adventure. I hear an echoing voice from behind me—it seems to be coming from somewhere inside or beyond the neighborhood's forest—and I turn around to investigate. *The fort! The fort may be compromised! What if intruders have gotten in and messed it up? My place in the trees...I gotta go find out!*

I run across the road and over the mound of earth at the entrance into the woods. I steady myself to not slip on the dirt-gravel that covers the slope down the other side. Pine needles line the forest floor, and I see my friend the pine bough, where I've spent many hours bouncing and swaying. I bank right down a barely made path towards the fortress, hoping that I won't find it destroyed. As I run, I notice all of the flowers and plants have shot up since the last of spring's rains. Purples and pinks and various shades of luscious greens flank the path, I'm careful not to be distracted by them so I don't lose sight of my footing. I leap over a gnarled pine root that crosses the path—this is the threshold I've deemed marks my entrance into fortress lands. My lands.

My pace slows and on my left I see the boughs of thin branches I've bent in a "U" shape to outline my fortress door. It looks as if no one is here, nothing has been disturbed. I approach cautiously just in case, and notice a bouquet of flowers has sprung up near both sides of the fort's entrance.

Bright yellow petals on fresh fleshy tall stems. Lacy white bell drops hanging from thick lime-colored blade pedestals. The scent of freshly cut onion hangs strongly in the air, and I wonder where the smell could be coming from, so far away from where cookery could happen.

I realize I am standing on some of the bell drops' leaves, that I have crushed them beneath my sneakers, and reach down to touch the juice that pools there.

Pungent odors of onion indeed arise from this liquid, and I hold a damaged blade in my hand. *I could rub this kind of gross smell all over the front of the fort to keep the intruders away! The smell is gnarly, it certainly wouldn't make me want to come closer!*

I quickly pluck some of the leaves and with one hand hold my nostrils closed, using the other to spread the juices along the bowed branches, making an arc from one side of the door to the other. I throw the leaves down and spit into my hand, rubbing the juice off onto my bleach stained pants. *Hmm. Now what?*

I step back to further ponder how else I can defend my secret place. It is then that I get called to the yellow flowers that have been waiting patiently for me while I forged into defensive strategy. I don't know what they are, but their delicate energy and fleshiness pulls me in and I sit on a rock to get closer to them.

I bend over and put my nose to their wispy petals and smell. I cannot determine what the smell is through the onion residue in the air, but something urges me to investigate their taste. I grasp the rounded stem and pull up from the earth, it seems to pop out as if extracting a hair from its follicle. I again attempt to sniff it, rolling the stem in my hands and feeling the liquid that seeps out. *Hmm. Nothing too weird.*

I poke my tongue out and bring the tip of the stem to touch it. A sharp sourness bursts across my mouth and saliva begins flowing in the corners of my cheeks. The flavor is strong, but not unpleasant, and I decide to go further. I place the stem in my mouth, its outer shell is tougher than I imagine. I roll it around inside, feeling its coolness and occasional drips of sour delivered onto my tongue. I then decide to risk biting down into it, fearful but also curious to experience a shock of acidity as part of the day's quest.

My teeth pierce through the crispness, and another flash of sharpness bolts across my senses. I chew, half-squinting, liking the intensity. The stem has grown stringy in my mouth, it continues travelling back and forth from cheek to cheek in its rapidly disintegrating form. I suck the last of its juices and swallow, hoping I won't get a stomachache, but glad to have risked it. I now have a new favorite friend of the forest: the sour-grass. I pluck another stem out of the loamy earth and poke it into my mouth, sucking it and letting the stem dangle from my lips.

The day has gotten warmer, and a ray of light has pierced through the forest canopy. It is greeting my feet with its warmth. I sit here, rolling the sour stem back and forth across my tongue, guarding my secret place, breathing in the friendly spring air. I close my eyes and wait for the next leg of the day's adventure to show itself to me.

5

CHICKEN SOUP

I am in a bus station.

It is cold and I have a pink dress on. I am waiting for my uncle to pick me up. I have a dollar bill in my baby blue suitcase beside me. I pull it out and flatten it to insert into the vending machine a few steps away. People pass by and smile at me, kind of. I press the button for chicken soup and hear the cup plop down into the vending area. A whirring produces a steaming hot substance that dribbles into the cup below. I watch as the glass door in front of the cup fogs up. The dribble stops and the door opens. I pick up the hot cup and hold it to my nose, taking in the savory, onion-rich smell. There are small stick-like noodles floating against the rim of the cup, amidst foam, and as I tip the cup to my mouth, the foam rests on my top lip. The warmth flows into my mouth and swirls down my throat, and I chew the noodle things slowly. I wipe the foam from my lip and look up, hoping my uncle will be here soon, before it gets dark.

6

Grilled Cheese Sandwich

I am standing on a chair in front of a stove. I'm in the kitchen of an old, kind lady.

There are lace doilies everywhere, gathering dust. The air is warm and the carpets in the hallway are plush and cream-colored. The old lady is holding a piece of sliced sourdough bread before me. She lifts the butter knife and dips it into the mayonnaise, and urges me to watch as she slathers it onto both sides of the bread. She sets this piece into the hot frying pan and places a thick slab of cheddar cheese on top of it. I can hear the pan sizzling, and the cheese is beginning to melt. She picks up the other slice of bread and hands it, and the knife, to me, and I repeat the slathering as she demonstrated.

I place the bread on top of the melting cheese and she looks at me, smiling. She reaches for the spatula, resting on the counter. I watch as she gently slides it under the bubbling morsel and quickly flips it over. My mouth is watering as I smell the caramelized cheese aroma dancing in the air. The bread has turned golden brown and is glistening, shining, from its time in the searing oil. She presses the spatula down on the sandwich and out oozes the cheesiness. She is explaining to me how this is the way to correctly make a grilled cheese sandwich as she lifts it out of the pan onto a plate.

She uses a sharp knife to cut down the center of the sandwich and hands the plate to me. I hold it and lift a half to my mouth and enjoy the crispy sensations it delivers.

I like this lady. She is a friend of my mother. I don't remember why I am here or where my mother is.

7

THE SCONE

I am sitting in the sun, at the corner bakery in the Diamond District of San Francisco.

I watch as life bustles outside on the street of this sweet little neighborhood nestled at the base of steep hills in the city. To my right, sits my uncle, he is looking out the window onto Chenery Street, he seems to be thinking about something. I can't tell if he knows I am staring at him, but I am, out of the corner of my eye. I look to him, then away, then back again—fascinated with the lines on his face, his settled energy, the contemplative look he gazes out the window with. I'm really happy.

I look down in front of me—on the wooden counter rests a white china plate with a crispy, golden scone upon it. Uncle also has a scone on his plate, already half-gone now, he eats it quickly with gulps of fresh black coffee in between bites. I try to look normal as I watch him, eating. It is still so fascinating to me.

I can smell the totality of baked goods in the air and smile inside as I lift the pastry into my mouth. My teeth break through the crusty layer and into the slightly dry, slightly moist interior. Crumbly sweetness melts on my tongue and I set the rest of the scone down, savoring, as light beams warm my face. Uncle looks over at me and smiles, then looks back out onto the street. I swallow this doughy goodness and take another bite.

Mid-chewing, memories of the morning flood into my mind: holding Auntie's hand, strolling past the smiling faces of old Asian vendors at the farmer's market, the glistening persimmons, the mist still hanging heavy in the air. The cold hard pew pressing the underside of my tiny thighs as I sat listening to Gregorian chanting at Grace Cathedral. How I'd look up every once in a while to what seemed like mile-high stone ceilings, feeling small, feeling awe.

The rustling of newspapers shifts my focus back to the present and I take another crumbly morsel into my mouth. I set the scone down. It kinda looks like a misshapen planet, surrounded by crumb stars, sitting there on that platter. I sigh. My time with Auntie and Uncle is coming to an end—tomorrow I have to get back on the bus to return home to Mom again. I struggle to stay present, with this sweet, quiet, safe moment, here with this man I trust—but find myself dreading the return home to the lair of Mom's heavy dragons of despair.

I force the dread away, pick the scone back up and take another bite, and Uncle pokes me out of nowhere, attempting to tickle me. I giggle and almost choke as I try to maneuver my body, dropping the scone onto the plate, swallowing quickly and pushing him back, laughing. He has returned to his silent forward-glancing gaze, pretending nothing has occurred. I push him again and he looks at me, smiling, as if to say "What?" with his eyes...and then he, too, giggles.

The last of the scone beckons me from its star-crumb surroundings, and I return my focus there—every so often looking towards Uncle in case he tries to ambush me again. I pick up the scone and before I place it into my mouth I take a big breath in—I want to remember this moment. The scents of toasty blueberry sugar crumbles transmit into my nostrils and merge with my taste buds' experience as I chew this last chunk. I close my eyes, savoring and surrendering to the possibility of attack, and grin so big I don't have to feel the future anymore.

8

POTATO CHIPS

I am curled up on my daybed. An irritation is peaking inside of me.

I'm trying to read my Stephen King novel, for God's sake…would she just SHUT UP???

The lights are bright in my room, and I have an open bag of potato chips at my side. I reach my hand into the bag and it rustles as I pull out a crispy wafer and pop it into my mouth. I'm trying to focus on reading my book in the safeness of my room, but outside my door, I can hear her. Like every night, she is screaming—at me, at the world, at herself.

"You're such a fucking bitch!!! The reason for all of my problems!!! I wish you'd never been born!"

Ugh. Etcetera. Etcetera, Etcetera. I've heard it all before, just another embarrassing night at the Lakins' apartment, Mom drunk and dancing wildly, shouting obscenities. I know she's just fed up with her life, I've figured that out by now. I can feel her desire to die masked by her fake smile every day. Still, her yelling hurts.

My hand reaches into the bag and grabs another chip. I can feel its waffled oily edges against my fingers as I slide it out and place it onto my tongue. I squeeze my eyes and try to focus on the *crunch crunch crunch* of my teeth masticating the deliciousness, but her voice is piercing my mind. I shift my body, placing one of my ears against the pillow, hoping that this will help me to zone her out.

The diversion is not working. I start to feel a burning sensation rising inside of my core, and suddenly all of my limbs are tingling with energy. It feels like something wants to burst out of me. Without thought, I leap off of my daybed and fling open my door, running into the living room.

The clouds of cigarette smoke are thick and the TV is blaring, an evening news anchor yapping on about something. I see my mom, holding her glass out before her small body. Her eyes are shut, and she's continuing to yell into the air.

"Goddammit!! Why the hell do you cause me so much trouble?? Why did I ever decide to have you???"

I walk right up to her, midway through her rant-sentence and grab her. I've grown taller (and wider) now, almost as tall as her (and at least twice as wide), and I feel her tiny arms in my powerful hands. My salty fingers are squeezing way too hard, and I feel my mouth open. Sounds come out with projectile force: "Shut the fuck up!!! Shut the fuck up!! Shut the fuck up!!"

I have never said these words before.

I am shaking her, violently, my eyes are tightly closed. I have forgotten all about the potato chips and the interesting story I was so immersed in just minutes ago. Something has taken over and I am now here, shaking my mother.

"Shut the fuck up!! Shut the fuck up!!"

I have never done this before. What is happening?

I feel the plush carpet beneath my feet, oozing through my toes. The momentum of needing to shake her comes to a rest, and I open my eyes. I look into her eyes and she is silent, her face still with fear. I feel her frozen body against my fingers' grasp, the edges of her terrycloth robe imprinted against my palms. For once in a long time, the apartment is silent.

I let her go and she turns away from me, almost sheepishly slinking to her chair. I am filled with guilt and fear of what has just come through me. I turn around, and scurry back to the safety of my room.

9

FRIED HAMBURGER AND POTATOES

I am sitting at the octagonal dining table in the living room of our apartment.

A hard chair surface presses into my bottom. There are three other wooden chairs placed around the table, but no one sits in them. The edges of the table are sharp, and one of the edges is chipped and is buckling up, a fake wood surface attempting to distance itself from the particleboard center. I am looking down at the carpet, a mottled dark brown, and the air is cold around me. I have a jacket on.

The TV is making noise from across the room, random people my mother likes to watch, spurting out facts about money things. I am focused on eating a fried hamburger and sliced potatoes, cooked by her. Mother is sitting behind me at the counter, drinking gin, smoking a cigarette, doing some sort of mysterious paperwork.

The ice in her glass clinks as I place bites of the spiced meaty patty into my mouth. All sorts of savory flavors swirl in my head. The potatoes are perfectly tanned, slightly burned at the edges, I feel the crispness on my tongue upon biting into the hot, mealy center. Around me, the cigarette smoke is so heavy I cannot smell much of the meal as I chew.

In between bites, my fork hits the plate and makes a loud sound that seems to echo. My mother is quiet lately.

10

PANCAKES

I am in Hawaii.

My mother sits across from me in a booth in the hotel restaurant. The walls are made of lava rocks protruding from a sandy background surface. Jungle plants wind their way around each lava chunk, their leaves huge, deep green and comforting. The patent ochre leather squeaks underneath me as I fidget, and I have a plate of pancakes in front of me, steaming. I'm so excited!

I can smell the maple syrup and melting butter wafting up from them, their scents dancing together in my nose. I imagine their gooey goodness as I hold my fork and impress a deep cut into the stack. The liquid oozes into the cut and pools onto the plate that holds them. I make another cut opposite this, now completing a triangle-sized bite. I wedge my fork underneath the triangle and playfully lift it into my mouth. All of the flavors and textures dissolve on my tongue, like spongecake.

Suddenly, the voice of the bully at school comes into my head.

"What are you, pregnant?!?" she says, and I see her beady eyes, glaring at me, her perfect blond hair hanging straight to her shoulders.

She disappears and another memory is here: me, searching through the pants rack at the department store, trying to find jeans that fit me. "I'm sorry, we don't have any jeans that large," says the store attendant when I ask for help. She isn't concerned, and there is a coldness in her eyes as she turns her back and walks away.

I look at the pancakes. I wonder if I should be eating them.

I look at Mom, how she's not eating.

Maybe I am FAT. Am I FAT? Am I enjoying food too much? Why doesn't she enjoy food with me?

A gecko is balancing himself on the lava wall to my right, amidst the greenery. I share this moment of struggle with him. He does pushups—up, down—as if to cheer me on in my joy of pancakes, and I giggle at him. I look from him and back to Mom, but she's shielded by her newspaper and smoking her cigarette.

I decide to take another bite. The steam from her black coffee rises into the air.

When she could no longer tolerate the intensity of her mother's nightly rage aimed at her, when she took a step to fight back against it, a new power opened up inside her being.

When she could no longer tolerate this rage—infused and served to her in the food her mother prepared but would not eat with her—a new awareness opened up in her: she could take in this food no longer.

11

DIET

1989. Fifteen years old.

Somewhere during my first years as a teen, I am invited by a friend to try out Weight Watchers, to see if we could lose a few pounds with each other's support.

I don't remember much about the food during those times, but I do remember how easy it was to cut food out of my diet, and how fast the pounds melted away.

It's interesting—and kind of sad—how many meals I probably ate during that time, and how I remember none of them.

I guess if taste buds have a memory, mine were protesting.

12

AIR

I am sitting at Denny's with my mother.

We've just come from a doctor's appointment where the doctor expressed "serious concern" about my weight drop. He suggested I eat some French fries and a milkshake and gain some weight. Just like that.

At the table, there is nothing in front of me. My mother's voice is begging me to order something.

I realize I have the choice to reverse what I have lost, as simple as getting a plate of food, but feelings of rebelliousness overwhelm me. I feel a strong and unfamiliar unwillingness to do it.

Something in me laughs as I look at her, pleading, while her black coffee, *no sugar or cream please*, sits in solitude by her side.

This would be the first of many meals of resistance to come:

Me, hiding food in the couch, sneaking bits to the garbage or toilet; throwing half eaten meals out my bedroom window; exercising excessively, stuffing pillows against the crack under the door to hide my panting.

Also interesting to note:

I remember none of the specifics of these meals, as if I was eating only air.

13

MEAL PLAN

I am sitting on the high school bleachers in the sun, eating lunch by myself.

I am happy, in a Prozac kind of way.

My meal has been precisely calculated and measured from a food plan given to me by my therapist and dietitian, whom I have come to trust and agree to eat for.

I don't remember what I was eating for this carefully plotted meal.

14

JUICY SLICES

I am in my friend's truck.

She is sitting in the middle between her mother, who's driving, and me. It is still early in the morning, the sun has just started to rise, and we are on our way to school. The truck tugs me to the right, then the left, as we hug the curves of the road jangling over bumps, shockless and rattling our bodies.

I watch as my friend pulls out a plastic bag from her backpack and opens it. The tart scent of apple slices permeates the air as she pulls one out of the bag and proceeds to chomp on its crispness. The apple's juices occasionally splash on my face as she smacks loudly. The smell is beginning to make my mouth water. I think to ask for one, but it is not yet time for breakfast, so I wait.

*A*nger and resistance began to build inside of her as she took steps to rebel and refuse the food her mother prepared.

She lost the weight she had let her mother pack onto her, the pounds that had been filled with her mother's grief and rage.

Anorexia tried to take hold as she restricted and gained freedom from her mother's control over her.

Awareness began to build as she met and worked with her first therapist and dietitian who modeled healthy behavior.

Confidence and hope began to build inside of her as she watched herself structure her own life to keep her mother's toxic energy out of it.

Love and passion began to build inside of her as she took steps to let her first love into her life, to have someone really care for her.

15

MCDONALD'S

1991. Sixteen years old.

I open my eyes.

Above me is a fake wood ceiling and a fan, blades turning slowly, a burnt out light bulb in its center. My head feels heavy. I try to lift it and it seems like a lead weight wants to pull it back down. I am in the arms of my boyfriend, and he's still asleep, but now he's starting to fidget.

The scratchy motel sheets rub against my half-naked body as I squirm to turn over toward the window. The sun is pouring in through smoke-stained gauzy drapes. This man next to me in bed moans and shifts as I move. He reaches out to spoon me, and I breathe in. I feel safe and warm with him, even though there are two of his friends snoring several feet away on the floor.

I can tell it is later in the morning, the sun's position rests on the carpet instead of beaming into my eyes as I lie here horizontally. I swing my feet slowly to the edge of the bed, not wanting to disturb anything as I make my way to the bathroom.

"Unf," he mumbles, "good morning…uh…where you going?" So much for managing not to disturb.

"To the bathroom. I'll be right back." I smile at him and playfully slap his grasping hand. He doesn't play back like I hoped—he's already dipped back into slumber, and his hand slides slowly off as I move away.

My body rises upright and I feel the room spin. I steady myself, hands on the bed, feet planted on the carpet.

Oh yeah. I drank a lot last night.

My hand lifts to my head and I sit there for a moment, getting myself ready to stand up. The dizziness subsides as my body does its amazing job of arranging things to homeostasis, but unfortunately it doesn't have my headache covered yet.

I stand up and walk gingerly across the crunchy synthetic fibers, trying to ignore the source of said crunchiness. I make my way around the sleeping man-boys on the floor. I almost kick an empty can of beer that lies next to one of their heads, but manage to make it to the bathroom with minimal sound. As I'm relieving myself in the kinda-scary-dirty-for-a-motel bathroom, I hear the guys starting to get up. By the time I've come out they're beginning the ritual of post-mosh-pit-battle-story sharing with each other.

"...so fucked up! MAN. Remember her losing her fucking shoe, Eric?? I can't believe you made us go back in that pit to get...oh hey girl, whassup?" The conversation has stopped abruptly for a moment, they're obviously still getting used to me being around in the midst of their boyish jaunts and escapades.

After a minute, they turn to me and continue, "You almost DIED in there man! You went down to get it under the sea of fuckin' people and we lost you. But of course, Eric nailed your location and did the he-man thing and grabbed you...and your fucking SHOE!"

I watch as they all look at each other and do their typical ending to awesome stories: wailing "WHAAAA!" and rolling around in laughter. How I managed to land myself amongst this group of rebels is surprising...and I love it. I'm hung over after going to some wild heavy metal concert with a bunch of guys five years older than me and my mother would be horrified. From straight-A loner good girl to this. No wonder she always glares at my Eric with her suspicious eyes whenever he's around her. I. Love. it.

As the guys recount more battle stories of drug-induced concert adventures and get ready to leave the motel, I head off to dress in the bathroom. Back in this moment of aloneness and privacy, I look at myself in the mirror and capture this person I've become: my perm grown out, feathery straight hair taking over; a plaid shirt two sizes larger than me (courtesy of Eric) envelops my shoulders; and underneath, a tank top with a giant devil holding a pitchfork in the midst of flames stretches tightly across my budding breasts. I am somebody's girlfriend, I am a metal head! My grades are no longer perfect, and I haven't counted or measured calories for months now. I'm not on antidepressants, and I am happy. The happiest I've been in a long time.

"Come on! Let's go, babe!" Eric is rapping on the door and urging me out of my self-reflection. I can tell his friends are cringing. "Yeah, BABE!" they say, laughing maniacally and poking each other, as I walk out and follow them to the front door.

We emerge into the sunlight, into the glamour of the industrial, seedy part of town. The guys sit down on a gigantic rusty pipe and proceed to smoke a joint. Eric looks at me. He knows all about my struggles with food. "Breakfast—you need it, Reagan. Let's go. See ya, guys." The guys roll their eyes at us as we walk away, laughing like tricksters.

The sun warms my skin as my feet fall into a symbiotic rhythm with Eric's, crunching gravel as we move. This is the only sound between us, no chatter. Yet the silence is...comfortable. Birds fly between the webs of electrical lines above us, chirping. A thumping gangster car rolls by, clouds of smoke pouring out its tinted cracked windows.

Just ahead is our breakfast destination: McDonald's. I am so excited! Never in a million years would I have let myself go here, with all of its grease and reputation, but with Eric, I just follow where he goes, eat what he eats. I'm here and (silently) jumping for joy.

There's trash on the curb up to the door, Eric playfully kicks it aside and opens the door for me, as if we are entering a fancy restaurant. And the way he does it, I feel like I am. He follows behind me and envelops my backside with his big arm, ushering me in gently. When we step inside, a grease-laden breeze hits my nostrils. The smell of diner breakfasts—scrambled eggs, and crispy hashbrowns—is sizzling in the distant busy kitchen.

I stand by Eric's side at the counter as he orders: "Two pancake breakfast combos and some coffees." I am trying to contain my glee as I think of the pancakes so as not to show how much I love them. It feels better to let it seem like I don't care and need to be somewhat forced to enjoy this.

He gathers our tray from the pickup window and there they are: hot, burgeoning boxes. My mouth waters as we find a seat and make our way onto the hard plastic, scooting to fit both of our bodies together on one side of the table. Eric takes the boxes off of the tray and sets one in front of him, one in front of me. I wait. He looks at me and I allow myself to open the box.

A steamy cloud ascends into my face and I take in the sweet, doughy smell of these stacks of deliciousness. Eric is already opening the individual packets of syrup and butter, basting my stack in this concoction. I watch him, my hands pulled back into my lap, my eyes looking up at his strong jawline, waiting. He finishes and goes back to doing the same with his own meal. There are no words between us, just these movements.

I pick up my plastic utensil set and tear it open. I pull out and set down the other utensils, leaving a fork in my hand. The pancakes have darkened, soaked with the syrup, and I can see deep pores, sponge-like, forming under this gooey liquid. I place my fork on its side and make my triangle cuts through the stack, remembering Hawaii. It was only a few years ago I was there, but it feels like a lifetime away. There, alone and communing with geckos; here, deep in love and eating with a real, live person.

I shovel the fork under the pancake triangle stack and lift it into my mouth. The familiar but missed texture hits my tongue and explodes with tastes. I close my eyes and savor it, this moment. When I open my eyes, even though it's been only a second or two, Eric is gazing at me, smiling wise blue orbs of gentleness beaming into my core. I feel his care. I feel his presence. I feel his love.

I look back at him and meet his gaze for a few seconds, then look away, back to the pancakes. His love is almost unbearable to be with for more than a few moments—so available, so here. I make my fork do another triangle impression and continue eating, glancing over every so often to see Eric at my side. He is eating, smiling, quiet. There are children screaming behind us as they run to their red and yellow plastic tables.

I breathe in and feel safe, complete and whole.

16

DELI SANDWICH

I'm sitting near Cannery Row by the ocean.

Huge chunks of broken cement poke at my butt through my jeans, I am balancing constantly to maintain my seating. Splayed out in front of me is the great blue ocean as well as all of its squawking compatriots, dive-bombing into and sometimes hovering above it. There are dilapidating canneries all around, leftovers from another era, a more productive time for this place.

Kaboom! A wave crashes in front of me onto the cobbled surface of abalone shards and pebbles, foam bubbling and hissing as the wave retracts itself. This sound intermingles with the sound of Judas Priest blaring out of my boyfriend's boombox. I can feel Eric's presence next to me—tall, looming, but safe. It is so strange to have this consistent male figure in my life, by my side, but I will not let myself think about this too much. I am just zoned into being present with him and his wolf-dog, Skye. We're all facing this great liquid mystery, silent.

Eric breaks the silence by grabbing and opening the deli sandwiches for us. Skye is trained well enough, but I can see that he's on edge with the smells and sounds of a fresh meaty opportunity spread out so closely to him. Eric picks up and sets the sandwiches down between us on the cobbled rock surface, then reaches back again to pull out a bag of potato chips from the grocery bag.

The crumpling and roughness of his movements rings out in my ears—him going about his business. I watch him, subtly, out of the corner of my eye—like Skye but without the drooling pensiveness. I am more in awe and captivated by his simple methodic ways of being, especially around food.

I remember how obsessive I used to be with food—calculations and ruminations and rituals—before I had met Eric a few months ago. So trapped, cold, lifeless. He seemed to exhibit no real concern with calories or ounces, or when he'd be hungry again or judging how much to eat. He just grabbed good-tasting things, ate them, and went on with his life. This continued to amaze me, even though I'd had many chances since meeting him to witness this spectacle.

My attention is pulled back to the present as Eric rips open the bag of chips and begins inserting them into each of our sandwiches. I can hear their delicate crisp surfaces breaking and snapping as he shoves them in. Like Skye, I begin to align with the drooling pensive state as he prepares this delight. Eric stops and looks up at me, straight into my eyes like he always does, and says, "Here," as he hands me my sandwich. I take it from him and, wordless, look back into him with gratitude. *He has no idea what he represents for me. He is the food plan/calories/control I don't have to think about. I am with him almost twenty-four hours a day, and what he eats, I eat. Such freedom this is, not having to think about or worry about food! About life! It keeps him healthy, he's not fat, he doesn't care about my being fat, so it's ok. I trust him. I trust him! I trust him with my heart and with food. Remarkable. I don't think I've felt this way ever with anyone. Is this a dream?*

My attention is called back to the scene as I feel the the sandwich wrapper poking into my hand. A drop of some liquid comes oozing out of the paper, darkening the sun-baked stones beside me. I lift the sandwich up to my mouth and place its entire tip inside to bite it. This is so decadent, but he doesn't care. It's normal for him, and he isn't staring at me like I'm eating too much or am too messy or greedy or gross.

My teeth carve a thin path through the dense layers of ham, turkey, and cheese, then suddenly break through to the crispness of lettuce, tomato, and onion. Mayonnaise spurts out onto my tongue. My top and bottom teeth finally meet through the crunchy saltiness of the potato chip layer. So very delicious. So very decadent.

Mom would never eat this, except maybe in the hidden shelter of her dark room at midnight. Dude! If mom could see us sitting here now, eating in the middle of the day and getting high! Whoaaa.

I take a moment with that thought, then look over again to this strange experience of having a person, a man, next to me. My eyes go past Eric and see Skye the Wolf Dog, his big, brown, furry body rising and falling with his breath—loyal, wild energies silent within him.

Eric, he just sits there, like it's no big deal. Like this all is not a big deal. Okay, I can sit here like it's no big deal too. But...it is! It IS! This whole damn thing! Breathe, Reagan. Don't show it. Just...enjoy it. Enjoy it.

My mouth calls me back into my sensory experience. I feel my brain reeling from the taste sensations combining and crunching loudly in my jaws. I also feel the intense fuzzy presence that the joint we just smoked is bringing on right now. I still am not used to this feeling, and how it kinda creeps up on me. *I am stoned. STONED, hahaha. I am thirsty. I am feeding myself. I am with a person who loves me. I feel my body. I am doing everything different from my mother.*

I breathe. I look out at the ocean in its roaring madness. I bring the sandwich back up to my mouth and repeat the bite-and-savor process again. *Dude, this is SO good...how does he not say anything as he eats?*

I watch him, and patterning my response after him, acting like it doesn't matter, while ecstasy explodes inside the totality of my being. The way the crispiness of the chips crumbles into my mouth, mingling with layers of bread, mustard, meats and cheeses...such a forbidden delight after my year of resistance. As I take this—and the entire mind-blowing experience in—I smile. Seagulls soar and honk above, circling in the clear azure sky. I close my eyes, resting into the moment. I jerk slightly as Eric reaches his big arm up and around my shoulder. He brings his other hand to my chin and gently pivots my head so my eyes are looking into his.

"It's okay," he says, smiling, our gaze staying steady for what seems like lifetimes. I lean into him, my eyes closing, and secretly sigh inside.

17

BBQ CHICKEN SANDWICH

It is after Eric's memorial.

I've been living at his family's home in Carmel Valley for the summer. I am sitting on a wooden picnic bench in front of the small-town deli. The warm sun tends to the coldness I feel inside, its heat releasing herbal aromas from the rosemary and coyote bushes growing behind the seating area. I take a big breath in and remind myself that I am not alone, that I am with loving people, that I can get through this—that somehow I will get through this. Eric's family is inside the deli and not with me—for some reason, probably catching up with neighbors who've heard the news.

"Gunshot...breaking up a gang fight...unable to find the shooter...pierced aorta... dead..."

I have received from them a BBQ chicken sandwich on a sourdough roll, and it sits in front of me, splayed out and sending amazing aromas into the air. A large, cold, pimpled pickle sweats its juices onto the plate next to it.

I feel safe staying with these people instead of with my mother and the weight of her despair, but am feeling myself beginning to restrict my food again. I am thinking about eating this sandwich, observing its crisped bread edges and syrupy sauce oozing from its tender chicken center. I search for my hunger, but it has genuinely left my universe. I am confused about whether to "push it" or to follow the possible wisdom of this lack of desire and go without.

It was so very easy with Eric here.

I have to eat something. I have gone without food for the whole morning, pretending to sleep until lunchtime to avoid being expected to eat breakfast. Confusion swirls in my head: am I "saving up" my calories to seem like I'm eating "normally" for the rest of the day—but still accomplishing restricting somewhat, like old times? Or am I grieving? Is this...normal?

I decide to eat what I can of this sandwich. As I bring my hands to the bread, I can feel the crunchiness of the roll as I lift it to my mouth. I squint my eyes as I tilt my head upwards to the sky and angle the huge challenge at my open mouth. The perfect sweet/savory balance of the sauce overflows onto my face as I manage to sever a bite from the toughness of the roll. I allow all of the flavors to blend on my tongue as I masticate the chewiness of the bread with my teeth.

I put the sandwich down, and although it seems like I took a large bite, it appears I have only nibbled at the edge of this gigantic thing. I wonder how I will do this, whether I actually want to. My stomach continues to be a silent companion. I wonder where my will to live has gone. I remember loving food so much just a few years ago, not thinking about it, all of this nonsense. I can't tell if my hunger is protesting my year of ignoring it, or if it has just given up.

I hear a bee buzzing behind me amongst the rosemary flowers. A slight breeze caresses my skin as if to comfort me here, alone, grappling with what my life has become, what it may be. I look down at the sandwich, sitting there with the tiny indentation I have made in it, and I pick up the cool gigantic pickle in my hands.

Its juice runs down my arm as I bring it to my mouth and pierce its tough flesh with my teeth, salty brine squirting onto my tongue in response. I chew and savor its coldness, feeling the softer flesh and its seeds rolling around in my mouth. I put the pickle down. I am not sure if I want another bite. I am not sure of anything. I don't know where I will live after summer, or whether I want to live without this man who so intensely impacted my life by my side. I think of all of the people he inspired, and, although I'm sure he had faults, how I never saw or heard about them.

Memories flood into my mind of the night I received the call. *Damn these memories...make them go away.*

But they keep coming: the disbelief, the ride to the hospital in the dead of night through mountains of misty fog, his mother collapsing with a deep wail when the staff informed her of their inability to save him. A memory of myself floating, or seeming to, amidst the whole experience, not really feeling anything, not really there.

I shake myself from these haunting scenes and look again at the sandwich. It just sits there, and a fly has come to investigate its contents. From a state of numbness, I watch the fly, allowing the insect's simple movements upon the bread's surface to calm me, to bring me present. Its little legs jerk their way along the bread until finding a sweet spot of BBQ sauce to dig into.

This fly, its simple hunger and need to survive, fascinates me. Does it feel? It doesn't contemplate this meal, I'm sure. I realize I am watching this fly for way too long and that I may seem a bit strange to passersby. I care, oddly, and readjust myself to seem more "normal." I decide to bring another bite of this sandwich into me, to allow it to nourish me, as the fly does.

Once lifted, my teeth make another effortful bite, and a large glob of BBQ sauce spurts into my mouth. I pull the sandwich away and put it down, almost coughing. I look around, kind of embarrassed, my mouth full and covered with sauce at its edges. I reach for the napkin lodged under the sandwich wrapper and quickly wipe my face. I wouldn't be worried about Eric seeing me like this...WHY do I care?

I navigate the mass of chewy chicken with my mouth, trying to swallow it without struggling, nervously crumpling the delicate napkin in my hand. I push the sandwich away, feeling done with the conflict. The pickle rolls off the wrapper in the transfer and I grab it before it jumps to death off the picnic table. I set the pickle down by the sandwich, arranging it like a perfect scene again.

I look away, towards the deli where the family is still engaged with the owners. I look back at the sandwich. The fly has returned, moving jerkily about its surface. I get up and let it have its way with the meal.

*T*he energy shifted inside of her.

*She felt the true conflict of her challenge
when she found herself faced
with the sudden death of her first beloved.*

*The anger and resistance she once felt towards her mother increased, but she
now aimed these feelings
toward God.*

*The energy shifted inside of her and she felt the true grief of having lost him,
the unreasonable need to keep going on
without him.*

*The energy shifted inside of her and she decided that she wanted to die to be
with him.*

The energy shifted...back to hating food, and life, and to Anorexia.

18

OATMEAL

I am sitting at the octagonal table.

I have returned to Mother's house, the lair of despair, because Eric's family home was too far from my school. I get to stay with his friends on the weekends, thankfully. We smoke a lot of weed together, which helps me forget this mess I need to be repeatedly steeped in. It doesn't, however, make me want to eat.

My back faces the wall heater, I have migrated from the free and breezy side of the room to gather warmth here. It is early morning, the light is dim, the colors around me are muted, grayish. The TV is off, far across the room, the couches are empty.

I am tired, and sit slumped over the bowl of oatmeal in front of me. Minute droplets of moisture rise in ribbons from its surface, and I look down into the bowl through the mist. Tiny clumps of oats bob up to the top, as if crying out for rescue. I have submerged these oats in too much water, making the mass more of a gruel than a thick treat. One packet of apple cinnamon Quaker oatmeal is my allotment this morning; adding more water makes it last longer.

I pick up the tiny dessert spoon and gently place its curve on top of the liquid, letting the viscous stream pool into the cupped surface. I've chosen this spoon specifically—I eat many things with it, its tiny portions delivering my sustenance over hours sometimes.

I lift the spoon to my mouth and slurp the watered down, slightly sweet oat water into my mouth. For a moment, I feel alive, my taste buds are reeling, my body hopeful. I close my eyes and swish the liquid around my mouth, letting it wash over my pleading sense organs. I breathe in deeply, and can taste the cinnamon despite the dilution. I savor. I pull the spoon out of my mouth and put it down next to the bowl. I am not really hungry. I am full of leaden grief, it sits like a rock in my stomach, but I know I am not eating enough.

I am trying. Yet this undertow of ritual and dissolution and numbing has taken over and I can feel myself slowly drowning in its wake, like those poor oats screaming up at me. I lift the precious spoon again, repeat the skimming, straining, and slurping-swishing. I am lost in the reverie of this hot liquid, these soft chunks of grain I chew a million times before swallowing. I look up at the clock. Forty-five minutes have passed, and it is time to go to school. I leave the bowl on the table, half finished.

Mother, sleeping, will see I've eaten "something" when she wakes.

19

VANILLA ENSURE

Sequestered to bedrest, I am only allowed to have liquid calories.

These calories are given in a specific amount to prevent any possibility of what is known as "re-feeding syndrome," where eating too much after starving for long periods can cause serious problems—and in some cases, death. So the liquid of this moment is Ensure—vanilla to be exact.

The clean, white door swings open and the nurse walks in. She is holding a tall, cool glass with this creamy substance in it, ice cubes bobbling on its surface. She hands it to me, and the cold shocks my fragile hand. I look at the glass—both terrified and wanting it, craving it, simultaneously. The nurse pulls out a straw from her apron and offers it; I take it into my hand. "Only half an hour for your meal," she says, peering over her glasses at me. The energy in her eyes is firm, but kind.

Apparently, as I had learned from other patients, it was common for people here to stretch the eating of a half-cup of crisp canned corn over two hours, and that the longer it took to eat a small amount, the prouder one should be of "resisting." This is a whole strange universe, this children's hospital and the games that are being played, but I am glad to be here. I'm so afraid of what would've happened to me if I'd continued to starve myself the way I was.

The nurse settles into her chair and stares at me—I guess it's time for me to begin. *She's not the laissez-faire type, ha. She's forcing me to eat, I get it, but I really want to eat. Do I pretend?*

I'm confused at what I should do. I'm confused about what I'm doing here. What if it seems like I like eating too much and they decide I'm not bad enough to stay here? I want to stay here. It is so safe and unlike anything I've experienced. The other patients seem to hate food, seem to hate it here, seem to want to leave. Why don't I? Do I need to act that way, too, in order to stay? Well, okay...I can do that. I'll take the longest possible time so I won't seem like I want it too much, so they'll think I'm really sick, so I can stay here for a long time.

Holding the straw in my hands, I hover its bottom edge just near the top of the liquid, ice cubes jiggling against its plastic, and begin to ever so lightly slurp. The cold, sweet liquid explodes in my mouth—so welcome are these calories, the denseness of nutrition. I revel in the taste, it is like Beauty, and stop to rest in between slurps.

I begin again and take another small infusion into my mouth, taste buds tingling. I stop and rest. I look at the clock. I breathe. I start again, savoring the half teaspoon of liquid, swishing it around my mouth before swallowing it. I stop and rest, putting the straw down.

I sit back and fight my urge to engage in conversation with the nurse. I want to know where she's come from, why she's devoted her life here, but I can't. I need to act resistant, I have to act mean. I turn my head to the window, pretending to ignore her.

I take a breath, feigning a sigh that should communicate how much of a dreadful chore this is. I look back at the cup and slowly move to pick up the straw again. I insert the straw into the cup, its liquid. The nurse peers at me over her glasses, set at half-mast on the bridge of her nose.

"You have only ten minutes left, dear, you better finish that."

As if I don't know, as if I am a rebellious child testing her. Maybe some part of me is, but most of me is literally, kind of embarrassingly, pretending. I hold the straw again and continue my intake, this time getting lost in the sensations. I do my best to both seem tortured and difficult, but also to finish in time so I don't get "supplemented extra"—an apparent punishment here. In my closed-eye reverie, I am surprised to hear the sound of the nurse's voice warning,

"Honey, you need to hurry up and finish that or you know what happens."

I am surprised that the time has passed so quickly and rush to finish—still with this weird pretense that I do not want to—until I hear air coming through the straw. I have reached the bottom of the cup. Since this whole restriction thing started again, I have become able to lose myself in eating small amounts over long periods of time. This was just another one of those times, albeit while being watched like a hawk. This never happened at home. At home it was just me, food, the clock, and silence. Here, with the nurse, I feel like I am more conscious of the sort of time warp I enter, transported back to suckling at a mother's breast (but of course not *my* mother, who for some reason chose not to breast-feed me). What just occurred is irrationally amazing, just a bottled liquid, my waiting mouth, a simple but sensuous intimacy.

I look at the nurse. The nurse looks at me. There is silence for a moment.

"Good. I'll see you in two hours for another. And remember—no exercising in bed."

She leaves and closes the door.

I look down at my legs underneath these clean, crisp sheets. I can smell the slight scent of bleach wafting out of them as I start moving my legs back and forth subtly. *I need to pretend to hate it here, like the other patients. I'm not supposed to exercise, so I will, or else maybe they'll think I'm fine. I'm NOT fine. I'm not sure WHAT I am, what is going on inside of me.*

As I pace my movements, I think about earlier this morning: me sitting in my hospital gown in line to get weighed, listening to them, these patients I'm supposed to relate to.

"It's so gross, and full of fat and sugar...I can't believe they make us drink this torture!!! Do you know how to spit it out down along your arms, into your sleeves, while the nurses aren't looking? Those fat ladies are so slow they can't keep up with me."

As I listened to this, I remember a nurse coming to me and wheeling me to the weighing station, past this line of resentful voices. I kept my head down so they wouldn't see that I'm a fake. In the weighing room, I remember rising from my wheelchair to step onto the scale, and the cold air of the morning whispering into my flapping gown.

The scale is also cold and is hard beneath my feet. I am instructed to turn my back to the numbers. I can see the other girls through the window, still faintly hearing their giggling and plotting. I can't stop thinking about the next time I will be served an Ensure, being assigned to take in its vanilla silkiness. I am secretly waiting for the next feeding, excited like I'd never been before…but looking at them I feel confused. Shame takes over as I compare myself with them.

About the nurses they go on: "Why do they have to go everywhere I do? Watch everything I eat? Stare at me when I'm eating? Why don't they leave us alone????"

I reflect on the caring staff sitting with me, always someone sitting with me, after all these years of solitude. How I must hate these caretakers, while feeling conflicted with wanting to absorb the deep nourishment that their attention actually gives me.

I must resist. To stay here. To qualify.

I hear the steel weight of the scale sliding across the notches, echoing behind me, measuring me, then sliding back. I hear the nurse's pen scribbling something on her clipboard. I step off the scale.

I am turned around, encouraged to breathe and to sit back into the wheelchair. I follow instructions like a good girl but with a false scowl on my face. The nurse rolls me past the girls in the waiting seats. I see Jenny fussing with her leg as I pass by, and I know she's probably trying to insert handcrafted weights on her body somehow to seem heavier. I turn my head away and look forward, feeling the carpet bumping beneath as I am pushed along by this anonymous nurse.

I want to side with her, ask her why I do not feel like the other patients, why I feel so confused, why all of this is happening inside of me. But I can't.

Somehow I feel like the more I share about what's really going on inside me, the greater the possibility I will be sent home because I am not as sick as them. I do not want to go home.

What's WRONG with me? Why do I not feel like they do? Why am I this pretend sorry version of confusion who loves this experience, savoring it, wishing it would never end? I must shut that part of me up. I must become STRONG. I must become like them. Then I'll need more treatment.

God! Even that statement, so lame! Why do I want to be in a fucking hospital when I could be enjoying my life? Oh that's right...I HATE my life. This is all I have to save me from going back into that hell. This, or death—and I don't really want to die. I guess.

I shake myself from the memory of the morning. My breath has increased and small beads of sweat are beginning to emerge from my forehead. I cycle my legs harder. The scent of the bleached sheets whooshes into my face with the repetitions. I look out my room's window to make sure I am not being seen, but also partially hoping I will be caught. Punished. Noted.

Just as I am thinking this, the nurse sees me, and is coming to address the situation.

When I put my mind to something, it gets done.

20

YOGURT

I'm sitting on the hard, hot cement.

My back is resting against a rough, pocked stucco wall, I can feel the little sharp bumps scratching me through my shirt. The winter air wafts past me, chilly, but this corner I have has a secret captured warmth. My legs are crossed in front of me, and on them rests a diet yogurt, smuggled from the fat girl's shelf at the group home. I used to be a fat girl, but now that I'm a too-skinny girl, I'm not allowed to have diet anything—but I am anyway. I know the tricks.

On the ground next to me rests a jelly sandwich in a Ziploc. I can see the moisture building inside the bag from its bask in the sunshine. A single napkin is underneath the sandwich, partially exposed to allow for a resting spot for my fork.

I hold the utensil in my hand, the cold sunshine gleaming on its silvery surface as it descends into the yogurt, tines submerged. I carefully lift the fork up and out of the creamy gel-ish substance. I make sure each tine is covered, but that I can see the spaces between them. It meets the requirements so I lift the fork into my mouth. I let it all rest there for a moment, allowing the saccharine contents to drip onto my tongue.

I pull the fork out of my mouth, letting the steel slip smoothly out of my lips. I place the fork down neatly alongside the cup on its napkin. I use the minutes I need to wait between bites to furtively glance around—a small, grassy hill to my right, a basketball court to my left. Groups of sneering or giggling teens are grouped on the grass, sharing lunch together. Sweaty pre-pubescent boys are yelling and squeaking their shoes in jarred movements on the court. No one seems to notice me alone here against the side of the building, and that's just fine. I wouldn't want their comments anyway, their interruptions into my goals.

It is time for another dip into the cup. I pick up the container and look at the yogurt's calm, wavy surface as I disturb it with the sharp spokes of my fork. I repeat the lifting, the checking, the moments of sweet allowance, and finally, the setting down of the instrument. The rays of sunshine warm my icy, furred skin.

I think to myself how backwards and miserable this whole thing has become. I was safe in the children's hospital, supported and encouraged to look ahead to a wonderful future. Now I have been relocated to a new high school and am living with terrifying "delinquents" in a group home. All of this is designed to keep me safe from my mother's rages, from my own suicidal reactions to her subterranean grief were I to live at home with her.

I think how foreign it seems to be a part of those cliques huddled there on the grass together, and how much I miss my dead boyfriend. I picture myself, pacing back and forth in my trailer park room back at the group home, listening to Wrathchild as loud as they'll let me. Music is my only connection to the ghost of a boyfriend that remains.

A loud bell interrupts my memory-trance, and I realize it's already time to go back to class. That's OK—no time to finish, all the more progress in reaching my goal. I lift myself up from the ground, my butt bones hurting, and I wipe myself off. I pretend I'm all done with the jelly sandwich (as if anyone is watching), crumpling it up in my napkin. I toss the wad and the half-empty yogurt cup nonchalantly into the trash.

I keep my head down. I do not want to attract the friendship, or jealousy, of others as I walk down the cold, dark hallway. As I watch my feet shuffle across the cement amidst the chaos of humans and their noise, all I can think about is getting back to that safe hospital, and the requirements for re-admittance I've memorized.

This keeps me calm, hopeful.

21

THE CARROT

I am in a hospital room.

My pointy vertebrae ache as they push up against the cold, hard wall. My knees are bent up to my chin and I'm grasping them tightly, hugging them to me. I look at my arms, at that fine downy layer—I watch as the blinding florescent lights highlight each hair for me. There is a commotion outside in the hall: a flurry of nurse chatter, monitors beeping, people moaning, sometimes screaming, and the sound of fists hitting walls.

A sudden cool draft violates my thin hospital gown as a nurse enters the room. She is full and plump, and wears a furrowed brow I'm not sure about.

"Dear, we need you to eat something."

She has a carrot in her hand and a plastic cup of some sort of liquid—water I assume. It's been two days since I was ushered here, and in that time, I've refused all food and water in protest. Now I think I've finally got them worried about me.

"….or at least drink some water…"

She's talking, but I'm not hearing. I put my head down to rest upon my knobby knees and start rocking, singing *lalala* in my head. The nurse says my name sternly and I look up. She repeats herself in capital letters:

"YOU NEED TO EAT SOMETHING OR AT LEAST DRINK SOME WATER…NOW."

My eyes swim with paradox—I hope they don't show panic, as I only want the nurse to see determination. I feel my mouth open and words stream out like ballerinas: "I already told you. I will not eat or drink anything unless you find a way to promptly get me into the children's hospital. We are done with this conversation."

My head returns to burrowing between my kneecaps, the swaying resumes. I know this is a crowded general psych ward, that they probably have no equipment to safely shove a nasogastric tube up my nose to force calories into me. Yet I don't know for sure, so this protest is kind of risky—I may not receive the bounty I've been resisting for.

The nurse is annoyed, and I watch her whip around, vacuuming a rush of air from my tented gown with her exit. I shiver. I think of the children's hospital, where they take my temperature and bring me warm blankets. Where dietitians and therapists and art teachers get it, how they sit with me to process the mess of emotions I experience when eating, when trying to live, when conflicted with this demon inside that wants to kill me. Before, I think, the rules and restriction helped me, I felt stronger. But now, look at me—pulled out of college and trapped in a loony bin with crazy people. This isn't making me feel stronger now, it's killing me, controlling me. Ironically, I am using the Anorexic identity to achieve my goal: to get back to the only place I know that can help me destroy it.

I breathe. My mind clears itself and I can hear the clock in the room, ticking, echoing. It reminds me of my heartbeat and I try to distract myself from tuning into it—I am terrified my heart will just stop. I don't want to die, I just want to be back there in those safe halls, where I know I will be saved from myself, from...whatever this is. Where I can figure out the overwhelm I feel about my fucked-up life, and why my mind and body are doing this to me. I lick my cracked lips, and my stomach growls. I hope I make it.

22

A MILKY WHITE SUBSTANCE

Consciousness first goes to the aching in my hand.

Something is poking into my skin, yet the dull throb must mean it's been there for awhile. I feel the slight upward tug of tape against the hairs on the top of my hand. The lids of my eyes are heavy; I am trying to open them but can only manage to crack them slightly. Through my eyelashes, I can see I am in a hospital room, and now the sound of a heart monitor comes into my ears: *ba bump, ba bump, ba bump.*

I wiggle my feet to see if they still move, and thankfully, they do. I breathe, and my chest rises and falls, up and down. I feel into the fullness of my bodyskin seeing if there is any sort of paralyzation happening. I can sense into all areas. I can feel the perimeter of my physical beingness.

I now notice that sticky pads are attached to various places on my chest, pulling at various areas of delicate skin and hair that has grown there. Following outward from this sensation, I can feel some sort of weight, of cords (?) extending out from the pads. Curious, I find I can move my head down slightly, allowing me to see that I am wearing a hospital gown that is tented in several places by these cords.

I settle back into myself, sinking into the soft pillow at my back. I close my eyes, trying to figure out what I am doing here—I was not in this room yesterday when I was admitted. I try to reverse the timeline of my awareness, but as far as I can remember, I went to sleep in a psychiatric ward room.

This is NOT the noisy psychiatric ward. I remember taking the bus, my uncle picking me up at the station and dropping me off at the doors of Stanford General. But this room, this is unfamiliar. There is no memory of how I came to be here.

I crack my eyes open again to see more of my surroundings and this time I look at the spot on my hand that first called me awake. I have a large IV arranged with delicate violence into my veins, and instead of blood or electrolyte fluid in the tube attached to it, there is a milky white substance flowing into me. I figure this is some sort of liquid caloric infusion, and I wonder how long I have been lying here. How I did not feel this getting inserted into my vein? Why am I not completely freaking out that there are fats and sugars and carbs entering my body without my control? Yet instead of the urge to rip it out, there is this calm as I stare at the tube attached to me, feeding me.

I pivot my head slowly to the right to what else is in this room, and I see there is a young woman sitting in a chair, reading. She seems to be waiting for something. I do not know her, I wonder why she is here, beside me. I slowly pivot my head back to center, making sure not to call attention to myself, and I again close my eyes.

Why am I here? Why can't I remember anything? At least I feel safe, unlike the past few weeks of starving, dehydrating, and running myself ragged to qualify for treatment at Stanford again. I have made it in, I am resting, I am silent. No more trying—I am here. Yet why do I not remember how I got to this room, who this woman is?

I hear doctors and nurses jostling about outside and the sound is so very soothing to me. I wonder again at how this has become my life, where I feel safest, calmest, and most at home in a hospital. The familiar smell of freshly bleached linens causes me to relax, and the knowledge that someone other than the crazy, fucked-up decider that lives in my head is in control—this brings me peace. Yet for some reason I feel a little uncomfortable with this situation, and this woman, waiting.

I decide to open my eyes and face what is happening. There is muted light streaming through the blinds of the window, casting shadows over every white linen angle. As I turn my head slowly towards the woman, she jumps up and comes over to me, carefully putting her hand onto mine. This is not a nurse, I see her personal concern for me. I look at her and she smiles, relief in her eyes.

"I'm so glad you're okay, Reagan. They said you died last night, your heart stopped, they didn't know if you'd make it. I heard and came as soon as I could. I'm so glad you're okay."

A tear escapes, rolling slowly down the beautiful curve of her cheekbone.

I still have no idea who this woman is, but she's told me why I am here, why I probably can't remember anything. I died last night, and I guess the life in me fought to come back. I never thought my control would end up in this situation, that I would KILL myself—I only wanted to do what needed to be done to qualify for help. How could I have gone this far, and what was it that deemed me worthy to come back?

I shift back to presence and look into this stranger's eyes, feeling waves of gratitude and love she's holding in her heart for me—someone who couldn't even remember her.

In the course of a few seconds under her gaze, something inside of me makes a decision. I was brought back for a reason: to help others recover from eating disorders. *I don't want to do this anymore, this cycling in and out of hospitals, relying on them to keep me safe from this mysterious whatever-it-is that I am traumatized by. It will be my duty to face my life and all of its intensity, to grow back my existence and to see what is in store for me. I will be an inspiration, to myself and to those struggling with this horrible, horrible experience.*

I smile back at this woman and relax. I feel the cool sheets lying lightly against my skin, and hear the rhythmic beeping of the heart monitor. I breathe and take in this whole situation. Something in me has settled.

I look down to my hand and let the milky fluid penetrate all of my hollow, needing places.

Things took a turn when she woke up in that intensive care unit, hooked up to heart monitors.

Things took a turn and her mother was not there.

This threw her very core into fear and shock that she actually almost accomplished the death goal.

She took time to contemplate what she'd almost done, and felt in her depths that she did not want to die.

She suddenly understood she would do anything to get past this horrible urging to kill herself slowly, and decided to begin the long road of recovery and life-long medication.

She suddenly understood that it was her purpose to recover and help others recover from this twisted and horribly deceptive demon called Anorexia.

23

THE RESTAURANT

1994. Twenty years old.

I am at a restaurant in San Jose.

Around me pint glasses clang, and sports TV blares with its accompanying hoots and hollers of fans. The booth I am in has plump, brown cushions, and my butt sinks into them. Outside, the sun gleams against the floor-to-ceiling window walls of the restaurant; it is cool and dark inside. The smells of fried food and beer hangs cheerily in the air. Across from me is my newish boyfriend. He's entered my life like fresh, life-giving breath after my time as a lone wolf in psychiatric hell.

This is a ritual for us—the college classes done for the week and now it is time to let loose a little. We are at the same brewery as always and readying ourselves for the same delicious meal. We are looking at each other, intently. I gaze into my boyfriend's eyes—they are green—and he has a sharp jawline that is sporting a bit of bearded stubble. He looks rugged today, and I reach over to his face and playfully brush against his skin with my fingers.

"Mountain man, eh?" I laugh, feeling the tiny hairs scratching me. He poses his head, chin up to the sky, and laughs back.

I bring my hand back down to my side. The waiter has come to the table. I order a pint of beer and my boyfriend does the same. The waiter disappears into the clanking, hooting distance.

"What do you think we should get, Reagan? The same?" he asks, his gleaming eyes sparkling at me.

"Yes...our usual." I sense myself already reveling in the experience, and I see that he is too.

The waiter returns with our two pints and sets them down, glass clunking heavily on the table's surface. The waiter takes our order: garlic fries, extra crispy, and a chopped Asian chicken salad. He gathers our menus and walks off.

Frothy effervescence spills slightly over the side of my glass, and the color beneath is a rich, deep amber. My partner's glass bubbles over and he is quick to grasp it and slurp up the head, sighing pleasurably. He has chosen a wheat beer, and a sunny slice of lemon is perched on the rim of the glass in accompaniment. I watch as he plucks it and squeezes it into the now exposed liquid, citrus mist exploding from its skin as he compresses it. I smile and breathe in deeply. I am so at peace now. He looks at me as he extends the glass towards mine, and I grab mine to meet his, the *clink* ringing out in celebration.

We banter back and forth, recapping our day, planning what musicians we want to see down the street later. I am interrupted by the sight of the waiter coming towards us, balancing the plates. He arrives and puts the plates down and smiles at us both.

"Please call me if you need anything more." He waits a moment and then walks away.

The plates are like pieces of art—golden fries, arranged in a precarious haystack, are glistening with the browned pungence of chopped garlic. The tips of each fry are deep brown, and I can tell they will be perfect. The salad sits next to them: julienned strips of cabbage, carrot and pepper, lightly coated in a golden peanut sauce. Atop this colorful bed rests perfectly sliced chunks of white chicken breast.

We look at each other, my boyfriend and I. Alight with excitement, we dig in. He stops for a moment and prepares his traditional dipping sauce—a dollop of ketchup, a squeeze of mustard, a shake of pepper—and mixes it all together. I watch as he picks up a couple of fries and dips them into the strange-colored concoction. He closes his eyes as he places the fries inside his mouth and savors. I pick up a fry and feel its delicate crisp edges pushing into my fingers. I reach across the table and dip my fry into his concoction. He slaps my hand away playfully, but allows me just enough time to score a dip.

I place the fry into my mouth. The smells of garlic, salt, and simmered potato rise into my nose. I bite down into the fry, its shell breaking delightfully away to reveal a hot, starchy center. A little too hot! I blow out in quick spurts to try to cool my tongue down, and reach for my ale. The glass rim rests on my lip as I tip it at a slight angle; the bubbling amber liquid flows, a refreshing creek onto my waiting traumatized tongue. I can feel the effervescence in my nose and taste the complex bitter-maltiness swirling around my taste buds.

I put the glass down and pick up my fork. We are sharing the salad, and my boyfriend has already jabbed into it a few times, crunching away. I watch him in silent amazement—even though I'm a little more used to it by now—how he just *eats*. How he enjoys, almost ravenously, and then sits back, toothpick poking out of his satiated smile. When eating, he is like a bull in a china shop, while I daintily pick up and take in each artifact, holding it aloft to see how the light accentuates its edges. To me, eating is a drawn out, slowed down wonder, every time. To him, he eats to live, and then moves on.

I pierce the disturbed bed of vegetables, careful to get a bite of chicken on my fork, and bring it to my mouth. The sticks of vegetable dance across my teeth as I masticate them, savoring the salty sweetness of their peanutty coating. A burst of tender chicken succumbs to the power of my jaws and lends a hint of savory brine to the mixture. I breathe in, close my eyes and swallow, smiling. When I open them, my boyfriend is gazing, once again, at me. He does not judge my artful appreciation of food—he enjoys it. I have come a long way from my fasting and measuring days, and I think that adds to the honoring energy he pulsates towards me.

I look at him, my cheeks full and crunching, and shine right back.

*A*rmed with her new awareness and purpose
(and perhaps the altered brain chemistry), she was finally able to focus her energy on something larger than herself—the schooling and preparation to be able to help others in the grips of the Anorexia energy.

Armed with this new purpose, she was finally able to focus her energy on something else than the constant counting of calories and fat grams.

Armed with this, a whole new life began to form within and from her. She felt proud and indestructible when she looked back at what she had come through.

In the end, another deep love found her, and the pleasures of the body came back to her world.

In the end, she felt such gratitude for being alive and on the planet, to have survived this struggle to be of service to others and herself.

In the end, she felt nothing could stop her and that the whole struggle with food was finally over.
In the end, she really thought it had ended.

PART TWO

In the beginning, she felt proud and determined when she experienced herself as recovered and in being invited to help others recover.

In the beginning, she felt this was all there was, that there was a demon to battle and conquer inside of her, that she would—and would help others—win.

When one day she met a powerful shamanic teacher, a new awareness opened inside her being.

When she was introduced to the concept of the wounded healer, of the rite of passage known as a Vision Quest and of the power of overwhelming sickness to call a healer to their path, an intense curiosity began to open in her being.

When she was welcomed into the possibility that there was nothing "wrong" with her, and how the struggles she had gone through actually were perfectly arranged to bring her to be such a healer, a new wondering about this "demon" of Anorexia opened in her being.

24

TRAIL MIX

2004. Thirty years old.

I wake to the sound of the drum.

I can feel the cool, solid earth beneath me through the thin padding of my tent. I see through my mesh window that it is still dark outside, and only pre-dawn things are making faint noises. I stretch out my body in my warm sleeping bag, readying myself for the day. I'm a little scared but mostly excited and honored to be here. Along with the drum, the echo of the night's dream swims in my mind—of that great Bear—and I know what I will "fast" on today for the medicine walk.

I have taken a weekend off from my job at the residential treatment center to do a Medicine Walk with a dear teacher I have been working with. This is an age-old rite of passage to receive clarity on one's next step, one's destiny, and I'm here with a group of people I've gotten to know deeply through my teacher's dream circle gatherings. I've told no one of my plans back home in my work life of my plans to do this, as "fasting" isn't exactly what a "recovered" staff person should be doing.

Yet over the past year, I have become heavily immersed in the study of animism, and of the parallels—the possibly sacred parallels—between the concept of a rite of passage and my experience with Anorexia. These possible parallels fascinate me. I want my whole eating disorder experience to be somehow related to this rite of passage, and to transmit that confidently in the eating disorder treatment world. But, as usual, its as if I'm living in two worlds: clinical/diagnostic and magical/spiritual. I'm torn between the two, and am keeping my thoughts top secret. In case I'm really just off my rocker.

The drumming continues, and now I can hear others rustling awake in their tents around me. I unzip my sleeping bag and slip on the day's clothes, sitting up straight and adjusting to wakefulness. I rub my eyes, grab the prepared backpack next to my bedding, and slide it over my shoulders.

I zip open the tent and I see her, walking slowly through the camp, drumming. I am so glad to be here, I am so glad for Whatever It Is that has led me to be among this group of deep walkers. The cool twilight air blows against my face and I squirm my way to standing, feeling the ground beneath my feet, holding me. I look around and see others doing similar things, but I know today I will not look to anyone but myself and nature for what to do.

I head out into the lightening darkness, into the beautiful shadows of this landscape. My feet crunch as they place themselves one after the other, the sand like broken chunks of crystal lining the path to wherever I am headed. We have been instructed to meet our animal guide when the sun rises: wherever the sun first touches my skin, whatever animal is present, is supposed to be the ally to help me throughout my day.

I have not been told this, but somehow, I know that the sun's touch will also signal when I can take in my first bite of sustenance. Judging by the darkness in the sky, this moment is a ways off—maybe two hours—and my stomach is a little hungry. I know I can do this, I have gone for much longer without food, but for very different reasons. I chant to myself: *I will make it my commitment to wait, not to deny myself, but to follow the age-old tradition of allowing the state of hunger to clear the mind for spiritual experiences to arise. I am releasing the comfort of instant gratification as an offering to the Great Mystery.*

I am walking forward now, fumbling around this place. I have no idea where I am going—there are so many paths that the fading moonlight is revealing to me to take as possibilities. I could freeze up and stop, in fear of making a wrong choice. But instead, I will allow my body to take me wherever it wants to go. Oddly, it seems to know where that is. It is as if I am being moved forward. I enjoy this sensation, not needing to know, watching where I am led, noticing but not being stopped by the small voice of fear that is trying its best to keep me safe. I give an inward nod to this soldier, yet carry forward beyond its reach.

As I follow my feet, I notice that it is cold here in this desert valley. I am starting to feel chilled—I did not bring enough layers to stay totally warm during this pre-sunrise leg of the journey. I pick up my speed, the crunching sounds becoming a rhythmic canter in my ears. I see the faint outline of hills in the near distance, and decide (or is it that my feet decide?) to head to the higher point of land to meet the sunshine sooner.

I wind my way past the edges of sparkling sandstone, running my hand along their walls as I try to navigate in the dim light. An insect of some sort whizzes by my head and I try to watch its shape, but its body disappears quickly into the darkness. My breath starts to be labored, my legs heavy, and I realize I am ascending, that there is an incline to this weaving path I am making. I again put out my hands, using them to push off the gigantic rock friends around me to keep myself going.

One, two...one, two... I count as I hand-walk my way up the hill.

I slip into reverie. Such deep silence meets me here, such aloneness yet such companionship. The boulders, wispy rugged plant life, the Joshua tree, the sleeping creatures...all of this, here with me. I take a moment to stop and close my eyes. I thank all of this life, I thank all of this being-ness filling my experience.

When I open my eyes, I realize that there finally seems to be a lightening of the sky—I can now see the complete outlines of the hills in the distance, hiding the waking sun. I become suddenly aware that it might not be long until I feel the sun kiss my face. I look around to see if I can spot a good place to head for in order to honor this moment.

I can make out the shapes of things now, and realize my feet have led me to some sort of canyon bowl, a plateau above base camp but not quite at the peak of the mountains around me. I see there is a flat area with a rock wall behind it, both of these things facing the east, so that my sitting there would position me correctly to receive the sun. I turn left through the tumbleweeds and boulders and make my way there.

It seems there is a perfect spot waiting for me, and I accept it. I slip off my backpack and kneel to place my palm on the earth. I take a moment to give a breath, an offering—sending energy through my heart, down my arm and into the sandstone. I turn my body around and settle into a cross-legged seat with my back against the rock wall. I look around, listening and feeling the air for signs of life. Not even crickets are stirring here, just a soft, occasional wisp of a breeze. I notice that I am quite warm after all my hiking, but know that soon, without sun and movement, I will be cold again. I unzip my backpack and pull out the light blanket I have brought, and wrap it around my shoulders. I feel like an old, wise woman, praying to the sunrise as I sit here in this valley, no human around me for what seems like miles. I take in a deep breath and sink into my haunches, feeling the rough earth poking into my jeans. I notice the hard support behind me and lean into the wall, waiting.

I feel excitement bubbling up inside, for the warmth of the sun coming. I only now remember that I will get to eat when this happens, too. On this long hike, I have forgotten about food—what I will eat, how I will measure it, where I will eat it. I have not forgotten about food for such a long period of time that this surprises me. I am aware that I must be in quite a sacred space for this to be occurring.

I am shifted from my thoughts by the spectacular sight of the first shard of light bursting, as if a star emerging from its bedsheets of the mountain. I watch it, this light, slowly creeping out and extending its arms across the valley's ridge. I am still in shadows but am fascinated that I can watch the light approaching me. I bring my cold hands to my mouth and blow on them, rubbing them together to keep warm. The light is creeping its way closer and I begin to see the colors of the desert come alive, the prickly outlines of its various forms cheering at a new day.

And then it happens: the sun touches my body. First my head, then my neck, torso, thighs, and knees, and finally enveloping me fully in its embrace. I close my eyes again and take in the subtle warmth it gives me. I am in such a calm state, tuning into the charge and vibration of sun-rays penetrating me. I can feel my skin, but I also feel thousands of miles wide, my consciousness expanding out infinitely. My body is still but for the rising and descending of my breath.

Bzzzzzz! Bzzzz! Bzzzzzzzzzzzzzzzzzzzzzzzzzz! A fly is breaking my peaceful meditation, and I aim to swat it away. It dodges my violence, hovers at my ear, and comes back to land on my hand. I go to swat at it again and then realize that this is the first life form that has come to me when the sun rose.

Wait...a FLY??? A FLY is my medicine animal??? For a moment I am irritated, and then I find myself breaking out in laughter. I look down at the fly and feel its twitching movements across my skin's surface. One moment it stops, then it scurries to a new location and rests there.

I wonder if it can feel the shift of my emotions towards it—from irritation to awe. I imagine the fly basking in my recognition, as if to say, "Yeah, honey, that's right, look at my awesomeness!" I giggle and Fly jumps, but returns again to my skin.

I breathe, then settle into being with this creature. I gaze at its eye surface, tiny bubbles of iridescent black, blue, green, and purple. I feel its legs, feathery tickling, each time it jerks to a new location. I allow it to tickle me and start laughing, laughing harder and harder as if being poked at by an annoying lover, and Fly dances around me as I jiggle.

It lands again and I look at it, amazed that it stays. It now seems to be staring at me. "What?" I ask, and laugh. "Thanks, Fly, for that laugh. I guess we'll be fun companions for the the day's journey."

Who'd have thought? A Fly.

The strength of the sun's rays is increasing, and I take the blanket from around my shoulders, shifting my seat and smooth the blanket down on the earth beneath me. I pull my backpack closer and unzip it to pull out my big bag of trail mix. I set the bag next to me and zip the backpack shut, shoving it away and to the side. Fly is all excited about this package showing up in the middle of Nothingness, and competes with my hand as I open it.

This is my sacred food. This is the food of the Bear, the Great Bear that has come to me in The Dream. I will not starve, but I will eat as the Bear. I will feel as the Bear, I will smell, touch, explore and travel inward as the Bear. I will listen to my gut and feed myself these morsels when my body tells me to, as the Bear would. I will not fast, go lightheaded, or go without to receive guidance. I will eat as Bear eats, having emerged from my hibernation cave and wandering the wilderness, attending to my instincts as they arise in me.

My fingers dip into the mix, I grasp a fistful and bring my hand out of the bag. I look at this food, cradled in my palm, then pluck out a raisin from the mound and set it down on the glistening rock-crystal sand. *This is for Fly, my companion. May I listen and feel and laugh with him.*

Fly is all for this action and has happily begun exploring the raisin's crevices. I laugh once more at my companion's antics, and then sit back against the rock wall. I return to staring at the ingredients in my hand—almonds, raisins, cashews, walnuts—their roasted salty edges brushing my skin. I close my eyes and thank all that has made it possible for me to consume this food, all that has made it possible for me to be here, now. I breathe and feel the virgin sun on my skin, how it makes the oil there shimmer like rainbows.

My hand goes to the first nut and I bring it to my mouth.

*F*rustration and confusion began to build inside of her.

As she took steps to try to apply this new awareness within the framework of the environment where she had felt called to help others, the inner struggle began to build. Instead of noting diagnoses and medications, she wanted to talk about her clients' dreams and parallels to spiritual emergence and awakening, but found herself unable to.

An urge to break free from the limitations of the mental health system, of meal plans and structure, and to find deeper reasons for this struggle took over her original purpose.

Excitement and hope began to build inside of her as she made plans to embark on a journey to get to the bottom of it all.

25

DEMENTORS

I am sitting at the head of a large wooden table.

Outside the sliding glass window to my right, a perfectly manicured lawn is beaming greenness, flanked by a multitude of colorful flowers. Around the table six young women are seated, three at my right, three at my left. In front of me is a plate with a delicious looking salad, and a roll resting close to it on a napkin. In front of each of the women, there are various types of plate arrangements—some have the same plate/roll setup as me, some have an elaborate array of perfectly separated items splayed out in front of them.

The tension in the air between us is thick, heavy. I know I am their role model, so I come into my strength and out of the spell-like condition that holds the tongues of the rest of the ladies at the table.

"Soooo, what movie do you all want to watch after this? I hear there are some good ones to choose from what Beverly brought for us."

Silence. A solid resistance.

"Hmm. Seems like no one is interested in claiming an opinion of the movie for the afternoon—looks like I'll be choosing it, which could be daaaaangerously boring." I laugh, even though I know these women are not thinking of the missed opportunity to choose a movie for the afternoon. I know what is on their minds: food.

Food, fat, calories, grams, cup sizes, ounce weights, the way their pant lines are carving into their "grotesque" bodies, whether or not they'll be able to feel the protruding bone from their hip socket this evening—I am very familiar with the situation. Although I sit here as a counselor, it wasn't too long ago that my entire existence was controlled by these thoughts, where nothing else in my life mattered aside from these ruminations, this ritual. I studied and wore this mask, pretended. I became this mask for so many years.

"Well okay, let's just talk about it then, shall we? This food is hard to deal with, I know. I also know you have all come here of your own volition—no one is forcing you to be here. So, what's with the hesitation? This is the work, and I am here to support you."

"*I'm* not here on my own volition—I'm here by bribery!!!" a young redhead retorts.

"Yes, I know that some of you are here by your parent's will, yet I need to remind you that you can still get up and walk out right now if you really want to. I'm not saying this to encourage you to do so, but I'm making you aware that you are still have a choice in this situation. Surely if you really wanted to leave, you'd be out of here by now. Let's all think about why *you* choose to stay, even if it seems it is your parents that are making you.

Something in you chose to get up and come to this table; something in you chooses to not leave out the front door. Something in you chooses to talk with your therapist about why it is so hard for you to eat, to care for your body and why you are tired of living this way. I know. I have been there. It is a struggle. To want to get better, but to be terrified of getting better and what that would mean."

The redhead picks up her sandwich and bites into it, pretending not to experience ecstasy as the flavors reach her taste buds. "Do people really eat *this* much mayonnaise on sandwiches? Gross." She displays a fake grimace for her audience as she sets the sandwich down and pushes it away from her.

I pick up my fork and spear it into the salad. I bring it to my mouth and taste the flavors lovingly crafted by our house chef. I make sure to look calm and at ease, as I know I am also in front of an audience that watches my every move.

"I know what got me to the table—fear of Ensure supplementation!!!" one client proclaims, looking around for agreement on the matter. The others respond by laughing nervously.

"I guess I *could* walk out of here, couldn't I?" another asks, picking up her fork and pushing her salad around on the plate. "But then what? Mom and Dad would just lock me up somewhere, or worse...cause they don't know how to handle me. They think I'm crazy and maybe they're right. They just want their little girl back, but guess what? I'm not her anymore. I don't know who I am. I'm certainly not her joy, her freedom, her spontaneity. I used to have *fun*. I used to not *care*. All that is gone now. Even if I did walk out of here and just run away from them and whatever punishments, I don't know what the hell I'd do. Ugh. I don't know what I want anymore."

"I know." I respond, chewing a butter-infused bite of warm, whole-wheat roll. I enjoy the rich flavors lingering on my tongue.

"Right now, though, the goal is to eat. The questions in your heads are so big that they are skipping over the task in front of you, which is to eat. Doing the best you can to eat will help you figure this out, although I know it seems impossible right now. Can we at least try to break the hesitation spell that is holding your hands and mouths captive right now and try to eat something?"

There are uncertain snickers at the far side of the table. "Yeah, a *spell*. Like sometimes, I feel like one of those Dementors are taking over my body...I can't move, I can't think, I am frozen when I am around food. It's like I'm trapped and I can't move. Controlled by the Dementors!!!" The laughter has a ripple effect around the table.

"Heh, well we all can see what movie she wants to watch," another girl lovingly pokes at the Dementor-challenged one. "You Harry Potter nerd!"

"Stop it! It's *true*! I'm so tired of this shit, I just wish I could do some of the fun stuff again—this is so fucking exhausting. And that really *is* what it feels like, so shut up."

"OK ladies, enough…watch the language. I have a reputation to uphold here," I say with an empathetic laugh. "I see we have begun to try to eat a little. Let's keep going."

The meal continues—slowly—but eventually it is completed. They know the meal timing limit, and although they push it, everyone manages to finish the food in front of them. I summon the ladies over to the couch in preparation for *movie-choosing/don't-think-about-the-calories-that-are-coursing-through-my-veins* challenge. They playfully push each other and fight for their spots on the couch.

As they bicker, I look around at this group of awkward but beautiful and courageous young women and I smile. Yet I also am starting to feel a sense of unease growing within me. This structure, of seeing and treating these women as "eating disordered," has been a challenging one for me to hold lately. I have been exploring an alternative version of seeing illness within myself, especially through the lens of animism.

As I look at them, I see highly sensitive humans who have been forced out of the typical high school drama, who have shaken up the seeming stability of their family, who have starved and purged and exercised to the point of near death, as if moved by some invisible catalyst. To me, I see all of these women as going through a spiritual initiation, especially with some of the dreams they have shared with me. I feel a knowing about this when I view how their struggles are actually bringing more truth, honesty and maturity both to them and to all those involved in their lives.

I know they can't see this, and that my explaining it would probably fly over their heads and make them roll their eyes. Yet I see it as so very different than nodding my head to the diagnosis and course of treatment laid out for them as I sit in rounds each week, discussing their cases. I want to help them—I've spent the last decade recovering, going to school and through internships to be here. I want to use the skills I've learned from these mentors.

Including here, at this place where I am so honored to work, I have learned so much! There is a sense of soul here: we have graduation ceremonies, we do yoga, we work with horses at times. Yet there is so much more, I know it, that is not being addressed. This new awareness is opening in me and it is really hard to ignore. I'm not sure why, but I've started dreaming of Hawaii, and feel a pull to go there and learn something about all of this. I know I have a responsibility to these ladies and to the team of amazing men and women I work with. But my soul is also demanding me to be responsible to it. Which do I choose? Can I do both? I'm not sure.

I shift my focus back to the boisterous giggles jumping up and down on the couches in the den.

"Alright ladies! Settle down, it's not calorie burning time! How are we coming along on the movie choices?"

They settle slowly but don't respond, still too taken over by the rebellious hysterics. The redhead fans herself as she tries to stop laughing. I let them be for a moment.

Although at times I feel like I am not that far from where they are—like I really am not the one to be guiding them while still having my own challenges with food, and this whole deal I have with diagnoses now—I am so very grateful to be here with them, and for their trust. I feel confused about what to do, but I am grateful.

I watch them fight over magic vs. horror vs. romance, and notice a warm glow rising in my heart. I may not know what to do, how to voice this concern and struggle inside, but I have come through death, mistrust, and deep initiations to get to this place—to help them, to see them, to be present with them. They are in the midst of their initiation, and despite my confusion, I can agree that my hand is outstretched to hold theirs through the darkness.

26

THE APPLE

I am standing on the edge of a lava-rock shoreline in Hawaii.

Before me, turquoise foamy waters crash against the black sharpness, and somehow gigantic sea turtles maneuver the swells without slamming into the lava's edges. In my hand sits an apple. I can feel its coolness, its rounded edges resting in my palm. The sea breeze wafts a piece of my hair across my line of vision, and I see an old rope swing suspended from a towering monkeypod tree, swaying off in the distance to my left.

I look down at the apple, shadows of light reflect off of its surface as the sun peeks through the ruffling tree canopy above. I have come here on a break from my volunteer job at the retreat center, and it is 3:00 pm, the time that for so many years has meant "afternoon snack time."

I have come back to these sacred islands to do an experiment: stepping away from my measured, comfortable, meal-planned, "recovery" life in LA—to explore my body's true desires, needs, rhythms, and visions. It is time to eat, but is it time for my body?

I check in with my stomach, my hunger—as if I know what hunger actually means. I have been eating forcefully for so many years for my "recovery" that I barely have any idea what that concept means.

Tuning into my stomach deeply for one of the first times since arriving to the island, I feel a sense of ease: it feels satisfied from the lunch I ate a few hours ago. I rest in this possibility that perhaps my body WILL guide me—that it *can* tell me what it needs, when it needs it—even after all these years of me structuring and forcing it.

I balance the apple in my hands, watching my bare feet navigate carefully over the craggy rocks toward the tree swing. Splashes of sea foam spray my face as I teeter on the coast's edge, one foot in front of the other. I stop, look out at the magnificent sea, and take a deep breath. A smile spreads across my face, a sigh escapes my mouth. I continue on, now grasping the apple tightly as my gait becomes unsteady over the edges and crevices of lava.

I reach the tree swing and it is see-sawing to and fro as if an unseen spirit is sitting there, waiting for me. To honor this possibility, I come at the swing sideways—this time on the islands has opened up so many possibilities in my mind. The swing seems to stop swaying, as if to beckon me, and I respectfully sit on its seat. From here I look out to the water, whitecaps dancing on its vast surface, and then down again at the apple resting in my hand.

The apple has no agenda. It does not care if I eat it or not. It merely awaits my decision.

My stomach feels the same. I could trust it and say no, waiting until the next mealtime at the retreat center. But for some reason, I feel called to ask the question out loud: "Is it in my best interest to eat this apple now, or to wait until my body says it is hungry?"

I am waiting for something to answer, not sure who I am addressing, and a voice comes inside (I think) that says, "Yes, it is best for you to eat this apple now."

Everything inside of me scrambles. The peace I felt upon checking in with my body, feeling no sense of urgency to eat, is suddenly thrown into doubt. I have no idea of who or what this voice is, and I begin to question whether it is the voice of fear or the true voice of my inner wisdom. Is this the voice of protection, of "recovery," warning me to not believe I can truly trust my gut so fully yet?

The old me would feel compelled to eat the snack, to stay on track, just in case this satiety wasn't real and just a trick of my eating-disordered brain. I feel something different now—or at least I want to *try* feeling something different now—to go with trusting my body instead of eating out of fear and mistrust of my inner sensations.

A mixture of anxiety roils in me at these conflicting messages. I finally settle on a rebellious persistence to trust, to go out on a limb and try to do this differently, to hopefully begin a course of my body and I working together, without a plan.

I look again at my innocent apple. I look to the sea. I feel myself whisper a prayer of thankfulness and of sacred offering. I lift my arm back and catapult the apple with great force through the air and into the wild and bustling ocean. I see it land, bobbing on its surface, in and out of the waves. I fantasize about a sea turtle coming to eat of my offering, but instead it floats and bobs and finally disappears into the great deep blue.

The energy shifted inside of her.

When she found herself several months into her rite of passage, malnourished and unanswered by the larger force she thought was calling her, the energy shifted.

She felt the true despair of her challenge when the dream of this all being some sort of initiation, of being led strongly to some sort of shamanic healing apprenticeship, was met by the silence and violence of the environment and people around her.

The energy shifted inside of her when once again, she realized that the thing she felt was most true inside of her may have been all an illusion.

The energy shifted as she found herself having great visions—of black birds offering hope, destructive but loving goddesses holding her; the paradox of life and death, love and hate—yet having nothing with which to ground these powerful images.

She began to feel unraveled and crazed.

True despair rose within when she realized that the only constant power in her life was this Anorexia, that food was not meant for her, and that God may not even exist. She was again left memory-less, but for several short poems.

HOW THE RAVEN ATE THE REAGAN

It happened one day

A day she can't even remember

Raven came hopping along
Into her world

Perched on the wild coast's edge
Mind swimming with thought
A cawing, a cawing

The old story
Of victim
Possession
Of evil and the fight against it
Wrestled in her heart

A cawing, a cawing
A swoosh
Talons piercing her
Now resting on bony shoulder
There Raven began pecking
Into her mind

Excavation
Pulling tendrils of old
Slimy bodies slithering
In beak's grip

Warbles of warbles
Sounds of slurping, mawing
Raven sucks them into belly

A moment happens
And suddenly
Streaming forth from beak

Visions of universes
Of voids and darkness
Of unfathomable expansiveness
Of good and evil and light and shadow
Merging
Of Kali, mother
Holding planets
As they build and dissolve
Image Nations
Coursing, winding, rooting
Into mind

A careful surgeon
A krrrrullll seals her
Warm iridescent feathers
Nuzzle

So close, teacher
Teacher, won't you stay?

As if laughing
Raven releases grip
Presses off the bone
Spirals back up into Nothing

Raven, aloft and Reagan in belly
Leaves a new waiting shell
Behind

Simpler Days

i wish i could
go back
to those simpler days

when i could
just believe
wrongs and rights
gods and rules
in my
our
sinning
fucked up
ways

but i've seen
too much
WAY too much
to pretend
i can
believe
these lies

everything's blown open
there's way much more
going on
those boxed up
understandings
rational
doesn't even begin
to explain
what i've seen
so what do i do
with this
these
visions
truths
understandings

i hold

can't shake them
they're swirling
inside this head
what do i do
with these
with them
with you

what do i do

this swirling

i wish
wish i could go back
to those simpler
simpler
days

know i'm here to do
show me

what to do
in this swirling
this swirling
madness
where are those
simpler days

THINGS THAT BOTHER ME

empty words
searing sunlight
blistering the skin
belly shame
jealous whispers
feeling you inside of me
without the thought to ask
doubt of self
losing me in you
lifewords sucked
vampires
alone in a room full of people
feeling what you hide
but not allowed to speak it
silenced
bone chilling cold
sickness when exposed to nature
confusion
overwhelmed creative flow
attracting needy
losing me in front of you
becoming the silent fool

for the longest time i surrendered
to the mirror
but now you're dead
now the strength is rising
how it wants to speak
now it wants to speak

pretending
can we please just stop pretending
i get so lost inside this stream
i am ready to be me
and for you to be you
tell me

what you're feeling
ask me
really
how i'm wondering

not just
these empty words

EMPATH

penatrative
penatrative
PENATRATIVE
i can't get you out
of my receptive mindbody
STAND BACK
GIVE ME ROOM
LET ME BE
me
loud
LOUD
L-O-U-D
i cannot
hear
the whisper
of wisdom
that resides
me
let me
be
you
in
my lower case
squashed
by your CAPITAL
arrgh
silence
let me hear her
whisper
whisper
scream

HIDING

Under the covers
Wishing for sleep
Heavy
These blankets are heavy
Putting form
To the weight
Not yet speech ripe

To stand upright
Play the game
Smile and offer
Niceties
Too much, too much

Lines of waiting projects
Ideas and identities
Eager to be embodied
Shelves and shelves
Of boxes and frozen choices
The center to choose
Under a wave

Where is the innate hunger
The urge to craft a recipe
The core to take this chaos
Into beauty and deliciousness

The sun shines brightly
The voices lift below, scurrying
Wills and urges activating, directing

Hiding
Under these covers
Wishing for sleep
Or the Real
To rip me out of this meaninglessness

So loud I cannot hear
What pretends to be
(What seeks to destroy Me)

WHAT ELSE WILL LEAD

So tired
This constant state of affairs
Waking
Hungry
Forcing the wait for time
Not allowed
Think I've got the key
Identity
Without this
Starving is the cause
Only tether to center
A me
Without this
Need to eat
For survival
To direct
There must be deep purpose
There must be a me
To hone in on
If not hunger
If not starvation
What else will lead
What else will lead
Ugh
This constant state of affairs

SPIRAL

why eat more
when so many are starving
why focus my energies
on pleasure, joy and nourishment

what gives me the right?
what is the real use here?

to choose to enjoy
rather than align myself
with the majority of our species
dying
hurting
suffering
starving

why eat beyond what's necessary
why do beyond what's necessary
why focus on this, my pleasure

what will it do for this world
what will it change
is my vision of holographic bridging
all just an illusory justification
to deal with, numb
the great suffering of the world
((the great suffering of my body))
if i make this decision
to truly nourish and focus myself
on this body
the only way i can justify
is to see
this flesh as a microcosm of the whole
and that by its care, nourishment
i will affect the whole

otherwise
what's the use
otherwise
i get lost in it all
otherwise
i wonder why it feels so fucking hard
to do what any animal can do upon waking
fuck eat enjoy
why is this such a fucking task for me
surely it must not be the way for me
if i'm not doing it for the world
if i'm just doing for me
is it worth it
am i worth it

why
why
why

DOWNWARD

feel like i'm losin my mind
can't keep my thoughts on you
keep driftin', driftin'

can't seem to carry through
staring off, into the space beyond
forgetting forgetting, the things at hand
missed you, left that, not here
feel like i'm losin my mind
feel like i'm losin my mind

am i
am i
or am i just relieved of past or future
am i
am i
do i need to control
am i
am i
plan
plot
list
make
sure

feel like i'm losin my mind
if i don't do something
will i forget you
will i forget you
will i forget me
will you forget me
will i
will i
am i
losin my mind
I gotta get out of here

DIFFERENTIATION

Wanting
Or
Thinking
I
Want

Going towards You
I
Am
Totally
Overwhelmed

Uncomfortably full
It doesn't feel good
It doesn't feel good
It doesn't feel good

Questioning
This desire
Is it trustable
Is
It
Even
Mine
Possibilities of permeations
Your projections
Leading?

You've always lead to Pain
nauseous
want to run
When filled
With You

Is this
somewhere

Off course
From feeling
Real Desire
A guide to
Nourishment
satisfaction
Joy?

Don't know
Never experienced it
It's all control control control
Why trust this
When You've always lead
To Pain

27

CHOCOLATE CHIP COOKIE

2008. Thirty four years old.

I am staring at the ceiling of a stranger.

I have come to this family's home to pet-sit while they have gone off to Europe for the summer. I have been here for a few weeks, and the newness of this place, its suburban perfection in contrast to the Hawaiian jungles, has grown stale. Once again, I am faced with a deep, heavy lostness.

I feel myself begin to sob, wanting so badly to desire life, to be happy again. My stomach is nauseous, not hungry at all, despite the late hour of the morning. I am confused at how my body could not want food after so many hours without. I am confused at how my body has given up trying.

Some part of me wants to live, but a bigger part of me wants to die. I do not know how to accomplish this, or whether to, and it scares me, these warring feelings inside. My limbs are heavy, just lying here, looking at this stranger's ceiling. Another wave of grief rolls through, and I cover my eyes while the tears rattle me. This seems to go on forever.

I start to feel anger rise up, like a fire in me, and suddenly I am kicking the covers off, thrashing my legs violently back and forth. I stop, bolt upright, and force the air out of my nostrils like a charging bull. *I am so sick of this! I have to eat something, DO something with myself!*

I sit for a moment, breathing, and think of what might make it worth it to move my body, to be outside in the sunshine of a glorious Portland summer when I feel like killing myself. I have no reason to kill myself—it feels as if this is a foreign being I am hosting. I am reminded of my favorite horror movie, *The Exorcist*, and wonder if I need that priest.

Suddenly, the vision of a heavy-metal magazine pops into my head, and of me eating a chocolate chip cookie. *A chocolate chip cookie! After all this time not eating, waiting for hunger to lead me, this is what my body wants? Not something "nutritious"?* I stop myself from judging, and am just glad I received some sort of missive to move me into the world. *Maybe something cool will happen. Maybe this is spirit finally talking to me and connecting me to life. Maybe.*

I realize I can go to the local grocery store and look for this magazine. I put on my shoes and make my way out the door to start walking. Outside the sun is definitely blaring—my skin almost seems to sizzle. I plod slowly down the perfectly trimmed quiet suburban streets, and I wonder how people live like this. I wonder if maybe this overwhelming desire to kill myself actually belongs to someone whose energy I am feeling in this neighborhood.

I stop my crazy thoughts and tread on.

I cross the intersection at the stoplight and make my way into the shopping center. I spot the grocery store and walk into its automatically opening doors. They *whoosh* behind me to close. Inside it is cool and dark, and I see the bakery sign lit up in the far corner of the store. I make my way there, and sure enough, a chocolate chunk cookie awaits me. I open the bakery case door and grasp its crispness, pulling it to me and place it in a bag. I feel the crinkly paper against my hand and walk to the magazine stand.

My eyes glaze over as I look at the long line of magazines, sneering inside at how most of them blurt out weight loss like neon Vegas lights. Ironic how good I've become at doing what the Western world seeks to do, and how I've done it so well, basically I am almost dead.

I move onto finding a magazine I do appreciate, and see the options are lacking. I guess I shouldn't be surprised, here in suburbia, but I really was wishing for a *Revolver* or *Kerrang!* to lose myself in. A magazine filled with imagery I can relate to, of death and ghouls, of fire and eviscerated housewives. With interviews speaking of the soullessness of our country, of making music to reflect that, to help people not feel so alone, to stir up some sense of anger and life force in it all. But these magazines do not exist here. I will have to settle for *Rolling Stone*, which fortunately features Metallica for the month. That'll do.

I go to the counter to purchase the cookie and order a strong, black cup of coffee, and the girl at the register looks at me with worry. I'm used to that look lately. I'm pretty sure I look like one of the ghouls in the magazines I love so much. It's been tough.

I grasp the cup from her and she turns away, flicking her hair to distract the moment's tension as we make our exchange. The heat sears my palm but I am glad for the feeling. At least it's something other than the heavy deadness inside.

I sit down on the pleather seats in the cafe's court. The surface squeaks as I fidget to find my comfort—I'm so glad for cushions to help my bony butt these days. I place the cookie and the steaming coffee on the table and sit back, the magazine in my lap.

I breathe and rest for a moment. I hope this cookie doesn't give me a stomach ache. I hope the coffee brings me to life again, gives me some sort of sense of purpose and vision. I hope that this magazine has some sort of synchronistic message that helps me feel like carrying on.

I reach over to the cookie and break off a piece, feeling its crumbly residue on my fingers. I place this piece in my mouth and feel the chocolate melting on my tongue. I suck the sweetness from the crumbling mass for a few seconds, savoring.

Then I chew. Ahh.

I don't know why my body gave me this image, but hell if I know what else to do with myself, what else to feed myself. The taste of the cookie evaporates and I grasp the hot cup of coffee, pulling it to my lips. I tip it and into my mouth trickles bitter, rich liquid that makes my head swirl. I reach over to break off another chunk of cookie and plop it into my mouth, feeling like a normal person. I take another swig of blackness and feel the cookie's structure dissolve on my tongue.

I let the experience take me over, and looking down onto the pages of Metallica, my body sighs in relief.

28

MOCHA

I open my eyes.

There are swirls of color coming into view, a ceiling recently painted in rainbows. I breathe in and feel the heaviness of my chest. The large house is quiet, the silence somehow seems to echo throughout its many rooms. Sun streams in through the window at my right. It's one of those unusually beautiful days here in the Pacific Northwest, but this fact makes the despair I feel inside even more miserable.

I try moving my arms and legs, but they feel leaden, weighted. I don't have anything in particular to do today. My life has become a series of purposeless days and nights since I decided to come back from the islands, vision quest failed, struggling to gain a job, and finally leaving said job due to overwhelming confusion, fatigue, and sensitivity. I'm staying here in this large echoing home with a friend who, out of the kindness of his heart, has offered this room rent-free to me while I figure out my next move. I have no idea what my next step is. This is an understatement.

I'm tired, I'm full, having no real reason to be. I know I'm probably underweight but am overwhelmed with how to train my body to eat more, to go through the discomfort of forcing down more calories to gain weight, and how to do this all alone. I tune into my hunger, but today it is not here. Often I control this hunger, but just as often, I am plagued by this confusing fullness and nausea. Where has my hunger gone?

I can feel the coolness of the rumpled sheets on my skin as I lie flat, breathing, watching my chest rise and fall. Feeling the sensation of air against my nostrils, my top lip. My chest rises...falls.

My head starts to swirl with memories of where I've been, how I've come here, and I shut their fluttering reminders down. They bubble up again. I shut them down. I focus on my breath, my heaving chest cavity. The timeline of my female ancestors plays out in my head:

Grandmother—diagnosed bipolar, hospitalized and given shock treatment.

Mother—suicide attempts, eating disorder, alcoholism, wrenching mysterious physical pain.

Cousin—successful suicide by gunshot.

Flashes of me, on the phone with the social worker:

"Your mother has tried to commit suicide again, we felt it necessary to admit her to Layton Pavilion. What do you want to do as the only contact we have for her? She says she has no one else. Is this true?"

I feel my feet slide against the cool sheets. *Yes, it is true. I have been her daughter, partner, friend, and parent my whole life. There is no one else. It has always been ME. But I had to let go, I had to let them take her. I couldn't handle it anymore. I couldn't. I couldn't. Here I am, almost dying myself.*

I take another deep breath, I let it out slowly. *What's wrong with this family? Why are the women of my lineage so tortured? Why can I see this pattern, yet not escape it? I have to take care of me, but this blood, these ghosts, I'm so tied down.*

I turn onto my side, curling up like a fetus in utero. I close my eyes for a moment, feeling into this shape my body is in, a deep memory I can't quite explain. A memory from the island, of my renaming ceremony, appears. I think of Raven and the Void. Images of black feathers rise up from behind, spreading out and then enveloping my back and shoulders. My agnostic tendencies doubt these wings, but they persist. I feel them. I feel them holding me. I cry. I wait.

And then, I decide I will try. I will try to face the day again. I let the thoughts and memories fade and I become present. Here, in this sacred body.

I start to think of the small things that make life okay, and the first image I have is sitting in Starbucks with a mocha. Sometimes, drinking a mocha will even make me feel hungry and courageous enough to feed that hunger with something good. I hope today is one of those days.

I look down, the sun has moved to a different spot on the smooth wood. I muster all of my strength and swing my legs out from under the covers. I sit up and ready myself to stand. I feel the cool surface beneath my feet, and rest here for a moment, allowing the blood to rise back up into my head. I stare at the sunbeams as they filter in, the dust particles dancing in the air in their midst.

At some point I feel the urge to rise, and I do slowly. I've passed out way too many times from jumping out of bed to do this mindlessly anymore. As my body adjusts, I move across the room to my suitcase and pick out something to wear, then clothe myself as if slipping into my face, my courage for the day.

I go to the bathroom and look at myself in the mirror. I stare into my deep, sad eyes and struggle to send love to that part in me that doesn't want to do this anymore. I stay with her in this gaze for a moment, then turn on the faucet, capturing cool water in my cupped hands. I splash this refreshment onto my face and breathe in, feeling the sensations tingling across my skin. I grab the hand towel at my right and bring it to my face, breathing deeply again. I set the towel down and prop myself up on the basin with my hands, taking one last look into my eyes in the mirror, pausing briefly again. I turn away from her and out into the hallway.

No one is home and I pass by all of the unfurnished, hollow rooms on my way downstairs. I grab my keys, open the door, and a fresh Portland breeze greets my face. I close the door behind me and lock it, hearing the lock slide its bolt into the socket as I jiggle the key around and clockwise.

For some reason, the sounds and visuals of things are very pronounced to me today.

I step down off the porch and begin walking downtown. The shade of trees dapples the sidewalks, their limbs and leaves dancing in the perfect wafting air currents. My attention is called to my footsteps. I slow down and feel each foot placing itself and rolling off the pavement as my legs move them to walk. I look back up and continue my walk at a faster pace, but still try to stay with the feelings in my feet. The attention to sensation is somehow helping to quell the despairing void I feel inside.

I reach the corner of the main street and watch as people scuffle about, seeming determined, purposeful. I wonder at this phenomenon for a moment, but not too long as to seem strange. I turn left down the sidewalk—my familiar path towards the entrance of the local Starbucks.

Each time I come here, a certain peace takes over, a peace I cannot explain. I worked here in the past, I know this place, and its recipes are crafted with repetitive preciseness—perhaps that is why. Perhaps it is due to me allowing myself to take in something I enjoy, something that makes me feel good. Perhaps it is a spell piped into the central air that lulls us into being here and paying for sweetened milk and coffee. Regardless, despite the judgments of many, I am drawn here.

I grab the handle to the door and open it, the smell of coffee dances into my nostrils. I step inside and the door *whooshes* closed behind me. I look around at people—some talking with each other, some busy on their computers, but nevertheless, at people living their lives. This comforts me, to be among the living.

I step into line behind a little old lady. She is next and the woman at the cash register greets her with a smile.

"Mona. Do you have your cup for us today?" The little lady holds out her ceramic cup, patterned with abstract blue dog decorations. The register woman takes it into her hands. "Pike Place Roast, no room for cream?" The little lady nods and smiles, then begins ruffling through her handbag for money.

"Here you go, Mona. The manager says that one's free today, so put your money away." Mona, still wordless, beams back at her and nods in gratitude to her.

"Bye Mona, we'll see you next time."

I watch this exchange and marvel at its kindness, even if it is company-mandated, and imagine how that little old woman might feel when she comes here—remembered, greeted, and treated with warmth. I kind of feel like that little old lady, so maybe I'm projecting, but it sure seems like she's happy.

Mona moves on and the register woman now smiles and greets me. I ask her how it's going, relating to how it is to work there, how some days can be challenging. She shares a laugh with me, but says that today is going well, that she always loves seeing Mona. I ask for a soy mocha and we go through the grande venti-foamy discussion. I pay her and go to find a place to sit.

I find a perfect seat by the window, in the light. I have brought my journal, the other thing that soothes me when I am feeling empty, and I set it down on the table. There is a book resting there, *The Herb Handbook*, and I take my seat and open it.

It is a thick book, with glossy pages. I love turning pages, feeling them in my hands, smelling the scent of each particular book as the pages are rifled. In this one, there are hundreds of beautiful images of plants and their Latin names and uses, and I find myself entranced by them, as if my inner plant alchemist has been summoned from a deep sleep.

"Raven!" The barista proclaims my drink is ready with gusto (fueled by the numerous shots he's had today, I presume). I come to the bar and look him in the eye, giving my thanks. He's a little taken aback, used to being ignored unless there is a problem with the drink he's made. I don't push it with my gaze, feeling the air of discomfort between us.

I walk back to my seat and place the cup down on the table. I scoot into the chair and put my hands onto the cup, warming them, and close my eyes. I take a moment to thank all of the beings and energies that made it possible for me to afford and consume this cup of goodness today, and ask that it bring me joy, inspiration, creativity and connectedness in my drinking of it. I open my eyes, quickly glancing around, a little self-conscious that others may have seen me do this.

I bring the cup to my mouth and tilt it to introduce the first silky sip between my lips. The ambrosia of flavors rushes my taste buds and I hold this first sip in my mouth, savoring it for a moment. The chocolate is sweet but also somewhat dark, a slight bitterness to it. The espresso layers this bitterness with notes of vanilla and glorious creamy textures. I swallow.

I set down the cup and look out the window. On the sidewalk there is a man with his dog, and across the street is a young girl with her mother, holding hands. My mind settles, and I feel compassion and great beauty in these simple images, these humans, living out their lives.

Although most of the time I feel somewhat like a witness—not like I'm living a real human life most of the time—I allow this feeling to wash over me. Something in me feels connected. Something in me feels hopeful. I am excited about the waiting taste sensation in front of me. I am curious about the feelings of interest sparked by the pages of this book that happened to be here (for me, I wonder?) I am comforted in knowing that my pen and my journal will channel and note all of these feelings and experiences I am having today, that I don't have to edit or alter or fear making anyone uncomfortable with the truths I write there.

For now, I am okay. For now, these moments are bearable, perhaps even enjoyable. I pull my mind back from the thoughts of what I am doing with my life, how this experience can possibly lead to feeling an overall sense of greater purpose. I pull my mind back from how I will possibly overcome this ancestral call towards sickness and death.

I breathe deeply, opening to a new page and take another sip.

29

PAN-FRIED TROUT

I have a squiggly, wet fish in my hands. I am crying. Uncontrollably.

Its slick skin slides out from my grasp, and it somehow manages to jump away and onto the ground. As I am set up so far away from the pond, its panicking thrusts don't manage it back to the water. It flops, to and fro, and there is so much grief in me I feel I will explode and crumble beside it as it dies.

I decide I cannot let it suffer anymore and search frantically for a way to end its pain. I pull out the fish knife in my belt and hold the blade edge carefully, thankfully it is still sheathed so as not to slice me open. The hilt protruding from my trembling fist, I walk up to the squirming fish and thwack its head, aiming hard so I won't have to try again. I squeeze my eyes shut reflexively as I make this jarring motion. I wait for a moment, listening, my arm reverberating. My eyelids peel back open, afraid to see what I've done, but apparently I have succeeded. The body of a lifeless fish rests before me.

I go to my bag and pull out the ceremonial cloth I've chosen to wrap the body in, to honor its life and the part it is playing in my rite of passage. I feel the scratchy linen cloth, and through it a wet seeping onto my hands. I stop for a moment and feel this body, this cycle I have chosen to put myself in, remembering the struggle and the blood of just moments ago. All is peaceful now, and I feel as if I hold a precious sacrament in my palms. I do. I am.

I place the carefully wrapped body in the cooler I have prepared. I close the lid down and take a breath. It is done.

I gather my rod and equipment and head back to the car. Things seem very slowed down as I walk back along the path that before held my trembling steps. I hear birdsong echoing in the forest around me, and although the ripples of sadness are still flowing through me, there is a peace that has taken over my body. It is a pulsing feeling, deep in my bones.

I do not play music on the long, dusty road back to my home in the city. I listen to the silence; I feel the buzzing, how it etches out the lines of my body. It is as if I am humming, alive, and I want to really be in this feeling. I hear the rod jangling in the back of the car as I make my way over the bumpy roads, and finally I reach the highway and head home.

I pull up to the side of the house, cars rushing by on the busy intersection. I choose to leave my rod in the car for now, and only lift out the cooler with the fish body inside. I make my way up the stairs and into the house—no one seems to be home, which I am glad to see. My next task is to cook this offering, and to consume it. Decades have passed since I have eaten flesh, and my mind is nervous of how my body will react. I am grateful that I will be able to experience this transition alone, and I make my way to the kitchen.

I open the cooler and a wave of slightly fishy aroma rushes at my nostrils. I take another breath, and remember the Fish message I'd received:

We are here to nourish you, if you call upon us and treat this exchange with gratitude. We are happy to offer our lives so that you may thrive.

I have to put this message on repeat in my head. I have spent so many years protesting and activist-ing that this message is still such a paradox to me.

I walk over to the stove and place a frying pan on it, turning on the gas clicker and lighting a flame beneath. I splash a little oil onto its surface and hear it sizzle. I breathe.

I bring the fish body over to the side of the stove and unwrap it, placing its cool carcass onto a plate. I look at it, looking back at me, through the eye of its half-squished face. These eyes are glazed over and cloudy, and my crying heart doesn't seem to react this time. I have become a little more comfortable with the fact that I am a killer.

I hover my hands over the dead fish and start to say my prayers. Prayers of gratitude for its sacrifice, for the worms and waters that formed it, to its fish mother, to the silky mosses it brushed up against and hid in. To the rains and the sun and whatever it is that made it possible for me to have this privileged experience, here, now. I wedge my fingers under the scaly underside and lift it up into the air, a gesture moving through me with no words. I bring it back down and into the pan, the sizzling intensifies, and I prepare myself to deal with the aroma of flesh cooking.

Surprisingly, as the fish body quivers and crackles, the scent is pleasurable. Savory, briny, smoky. My stomach begins to rumble. *My stomach begins to rumble! My stomach hasn't rumbled in what seems like...decades.*

I am curious, and my mouth starts to water.

I grasp the spatula from its peg near the chopping block, and pry up the crisped skin of the fish body from the hot pan. I maneuver it somehow so that, in one fell swoop, I manage to flip it over onto its other side without a mess. It plops back and resumes its sizzle.

I am calm, reminding myself of the message. Guilt and fear try to creep into the edges of this experience, but the unbelievable fullness of the sacred overwhelms their tries. I look at the fish eyes again, and it seems the mouth is now smiling. The metalhead inside me chuckles at the grimness of a slightly smashed fish head smiling.

The aromas have taken over the air in the kitchen. I'm not sure whether or not the fish is ready, but it is now beginning to burn, so I remove it from the flame. I pull open the drawer next to the stove and pull out a fork, curious to see what it will look like, surprised again at the ease with which I've transitioned into this meat-eater persona.

I pierce the crispy flesh and pry into the muscle. I see it has hardened and its texture reminds me of fish-and-chips of so long ago. I decide it is ready, and remove the fork.

I slide the fish onto a plate and brace myself for the big moment. I breathe, body quaking again. The tremble has returned for some reason, and it makes my fork wiggle. I am called back to the wriggling of the fish, in my hands, on that mossy earth, dying, and how it's now here, cooked, and on my plate. I feel tears well up, but they do not escape the rims of my eyelids, they just pool there. I lower my shaking fork down into the flesh of this dear creature, and lift a chunk of its cooked body up to my eye level. I look at it, fearing, but also in utter awe.

I place the fish in my mouth and close my lips around it. I slide the fork tines out and feel the saliva pooling around this new foodstuff placed there. All sorts of salty notes trickle around the sides of my cheeks as I begin to chew this strange, flaky texture. I close my eyes and breathe in, noting this ending of the rite it has taken so long to complete.

The tastes swirl in my head, and my stomach—and soul—is sated. I have received.

*T*hings took a turn.

When she found a community of others who saw her struggle in much deeper ways, that wanted to hear her story, things took a turn. She suddenly understood that this "demon" she'd been trying to fight was actually an inner shadow sister begging for her attention.

Things took a turn when she found that the initiation she had expected to happen in months actually took decades to pass through.

Things took a turn when she suddenly understood that she may have been on the shamanic journey...the Underworld Journey...all along.

Things took a turn when she suddenly understood that maybe her body, and her relationship with food, was guiding her to a deep healing of her innermost realms.

Things took a turn when she found the mythology of the Descent of Inanna, who travels into the Underworld to be with, not battle, her rageful sister. She suddenly understood her story, her struggles with death and body and food, in a new light.

30

HOT CEREAL

2011. Thirty seven years old.

I am sitting on a long, wooden table.

I am looking out into the yard through a large rectangular window to my right. The first rays of morning light peek through clouds and onto my face. In its wake, crisp frost sparkles on grass and rooftops.

My legs are stretched out along the table's length. The table has been repurposed for a seat in the common area of this communal living home. In my lap rests a bowl of oatmeal, its steam wafts into my face as I cradle the bowl's warmth with my hands. I look at its surface, chunky and reflecting an oily sheen.

This is no diet oatmeal, of days long ago. This is a weight-gain cereal, prescribed by my most recent dietitian to help me start putting on weight lost from my last bed-ridden flu episode. Laden with grains, coconut oil and almond butter, it is sure to awaken the "too full" demons inside me, but I am committed. This dietitian is like no other I have worked with.

I grasp the spoon, now warmed from sitting in the heated gruel, and lift some of the chunky mass up into my mouth. Rich sensations of nuttiness and creamy coconut slide across my taste buds. I hold the contents in my mouth out of habit. Tiny gel-like seeds swish around my tongue as I pulse the morsels with my cheeks and suck the goodness out of them. Finally, I chew and swallow. I can feel the tepid contents slither down my throat and into my stomach.

I am nervous, very nervous. Not because I will gain weight. Not because of fat grams, or calories, or glutens or whatever. I am nervous because I am already full. I have been eating my prescribed meals for the past few days and I think my gas tank is ready to burst. I have been here before, way too often, and know it takes time for my body to readjust to a new caloric level after reducing my food intake, but every time this feeling stops me. I marvel at people who like the feeling of fullness. To me it feels like terror and that something very, very wrong is happening.

I take another bite and do my best to savor the slimy concoction. I am trying to remember the voice of my dietitian/high priestess/kitchen witch in my head:

Hello, Beautiful. This will be hard, for you are dancing with the Dark Sister in your time in the Underworld. Know that you, as Inanna, can and will survive this, but you must first endure the suffering. May it not be long, but know that with each morsel of Love that you feed yourself, the Dark Sister will kick and scream. She is in you, as well as is your Love. It is your job to feed Her with kindness anyway, set boundaries with Her, but also respect Her as a part of you, as a part of this life we live in a body. She has great teachings to offer, as do you. And remember! You have come so far, your moon has appeared, Her blood has blessed you for your efforts to gain more mass in the world. Keep going. My prayers to you in this challenging time...

After a few more mouthfuls, I begin to feel the familiar nausea. The aromas of coconut no longer entice me, instead I feel a gag rising in my throat. I look down at the half-eaten bowl of cereal, resting for a moment. A sudden cramp jars my contemplation, and I set the bowl down. I place my hand on my stomach and bend over, hoping the pain will pass soon, but I know I am probably in for a long enduring.

It is a dull ache, and I rock, back and forth, holding myself through it. It is still early enough for privacy to be possible here, yet I hope no one walks into the common area to witness me like this. No one in the community knows I struggle with food in this way. I have held my history like a forbidden jewel—and shame—for many years. I don't even know what I would say if someone were to walk through that door and ask me to describe what really was happening in me. I've smiled and pretended like everything's okay for way too long to remember how to speak the words of vulnerability.

After subsiding for a moment, another cramp weaves through my digestive tract, and now I can feel a big lump in my throat. I try swallowing to make it go away, but it persists. I look at the bowl of cereal, and the nausea screams for me to stop eating. Yet I have committed.

I pick up the bowl and set it back into my lap. By now the cereal has congealed into a more solid, less soupy form. The spoon sticks out of it, and I grab it in protest against this part of me that wants to throw the bowl and its contents against the wall. I place a clump of lukewarm cereal into my mouth and chew whilst resisting my gag reflex.

I wonder why it is so somatically difficult for me to eat "more," why most people seem to revel in and look forward to the feeling of fullness, of why others don't have this horrible confusing cramping/can't you see I need you to stop eating/but-I'm-starving/so keep going/but stop/but keep going kind of feeling when eating more than their usual amount of food? Why does it hurt, physically hurt, to eat when my body "needs" it? How did I go from a food-loving child to this strange conglomeration of painful sensations whenever eating more than just enough to survive?

Once more, I try to remember her words of support, try to bring them into my mind as I struggle. I chew and swallow, chew and swallow, until the cereal is finally gone. I place the bowl down on the fake wood surface of the table-chair. I turn my head to look out the window, hoping to distract myself. The sun has fully emerged from its cloud horizon and I let the stream of warmth soothe my face.

I can do this, but OW! Another cramp ripples through my system. I wrap the blanket that's been supporting my back up and around me, like a sick old lady and resume rocking, back and forth. I don't care if anyone sees me now, I am in too much pain to care. Nausea and hints of stomach acid start burbling in the back of my throat. My body wants to hurl but I swallow it down.

I am so confused by this Dark Sister inside of me. I have come to like this name I now use for Anorexia. The myth of Inanna helps me to hold on and feel like I am living an age-old cycle of initiation (not insanity) in this process. In the underworld with My Dark Sister, I am staring into Her, trying to reflect love back to Her, trying not to slay or dominate or fight Her as so many have tried before. I am trying to love Her, yet also keep myself from starving on Her hook. She isn't sure about me, I know it. She screams and hollers how She hates me for what I am doing to Her, trying with all Her might to prevent me from thriving.

Yet I am committed. I am committed to feeding Her Love, to showing Her a different way, and to helping Her understand that to kill me would mean she, too, would perish—and that both of us, Dark and Light, have things to offer this world. Initiation, Heroine's Journey, Sacred Underworld Teachings, Blood Mysteries, Dancing with the Dark and the Brilliance...

I rock, rock, rock, thinking of these things, of my commitment to Love, while the next cramp and wave of nausea rolls through. The sun now warms my back as I grasp my knees, doubling over into a ball. I embrace this confused, confused body to my heart and wait for time to pass.

*T*hings took a turn.

Things took a turn when she once again lost all that she knew to an uncontrollable force both inside and outside of her.

Things took a turn
when she found herself on her way back to treatment.

31

TUNA WRAP

2015. Forty one years old.

I am sitting at a small wobbly table next to a sliding glass door.

Beyond the glass there is a tiny porch that looks out onto a cemented hotel courtyard. Above the outlines of the hotel roof, the sky is blue. Imported palm trees stand still in the windless atmosphere.

In front of me is a tuna wrap I have just purchased from Trader Joe's. Or rather, only one half of it is still a wrap. I have taken one of the halves and unrolled it to expose its chunky, fishy interior and to begin my process of consuming it as methodically, as slowly as I can.

A fork is in my hand. I use it to scoop up a small portion of the creamy mass into my mouth. Chunks of tuna flesh and onion hit my senses, savory and pungent, their textures compressing between my teeth as I chew, chew, chew.

I put the fork down between each of these bites until finally the innards are gone, leaving a somewhat soggy, flat tortilla shell exposed. I pick up the fork again in one hand, a knife in the other. A gleam of light reflects off their silvery surfaces as I position them for surgery, to start cutting up this wheaty layer into sections.

This is my favorite part, so I save it for last.

The fork pierces the doughy tortilla and holds it in place as I use the knife to separate it into double-digit pieces. I set the knife down. The fork lifts up the first section of tortilla into my mouth. I let it rest on my tongue, allowing its grainy deliciousness to dissolve there. I put the fork down, and settle into this savoring and waiting process, until it is time to take the next bite.

I look around at my environment, taking in the perfectly made bed, its smoothed and crisped edges. While I was away at Trader Joe's, the underpaid housekeepers must have made their daily visit. I remember being on a housekeeping team myself a few weeks ago before all of this happened. How is it that I am here, and that all of that life is…gone? I look at the furniture surfaces, clear of dust, and admire their struggle to shine even in the dim light I have chosen to keep in the room.

I have come to this place as a refuge from the fire, and a part of me feels grateful. The basic necessities in my external world are being cared for. I lost no pets, friends or living things in its wake. Yet another part of me is weighted down by total and utter despair. It took everything, this fire—my home of six years, my place of employment, my community, my truck—and now I am here, left feeling untethered, lost, wandering for meaning.

Granted, this isn't a novel feeling. I've known for a while now that living in community has only distracted me from the familiar depression I've felt for most of my life. Now I'm left staring into it deeply, no distractions between us.

Once again, I am here with it, and I have no idea where I'll go. After the FEMA resources move me on from this hotel, I've no idea where I'll live or how I will survive. The entire community has scurried away to their respective burrows to live out the trauma in their own ways. And while I felt close to some of them, I am in no way prepared to reveal the level of vulnerability and madness I feel. I've contacted no one, made no efforts to reach out. I fear showing what I've become; I fear that I, too, would contract their despair if I drew near them. And so, I am here, in this dark hotel room, alone.

A familiar feeling has risen in the past month since the disaster, one that I haven't felt in a very long time. Since no other purpose, connection, reason or meaning seems to guide me, I am feeling the desire to starve my way back to treatment again. To go through this old, old ritual in hopes of finding help, a team of people who can help me figure out what the hell to do with my life—to help me figure out what the hell I'm *doing* with my life, needing to starve like this again.

Why I cannot pull myself up by the bootstraps and "deal with it"—why I cannot be a strong inspiration to others, using the time to travel and revel in my "freedom"—is beyond me. Instead, I feel incapacitated, frozen, finding myself crying uncontrollably and unpredictably several times daily. I am ravenous, and then nauseous and on the edge of vomiting all within minutes. I am cold, tired. I feel so confused at what my body wants, why it is feeling so intensely. Why is it that all I can do is get myself out of bed, put on some clothing, and walk around the block? I find myself lying sideways, for hours, in the tepid water of the hotel bathtub, staring into its cold white porcelain.

Why is this all I can do?

Sitting here with the "wrap" before me, I look at what's left of my allowed portion. One-half equals 300 calories. This is all I can have in order to continue my work to qualify for treatment. I've been trying for the past few weeks, but I still am "too healthy" for insurance to deem inpatient (or even day treatment) necessary. My hair is falling out, I'm cold all of the time, my menses have stopped for over six months now, and my pulse has slowed to fifty-nine bpm, but I'm still "too healthy." It's a sad, familiar truth, the dealing with this system. But I know how to play that game, however fucked up I feel playing it. I know how to qualify.

This has become my post-disaster world: carefully measured meals, waiting out hunger, fasting for days before doctor's appointments I have carefully arranged. Repeated lab-work, vitals and weighing, hoping for emergency values to prove I need help to the powers that be. Talking to "professionals" who have no idea what the hell to do with me besides recommend medication.

Waiting in mental health facilities for screenings, while shouting people wrestle behind locked doors—wondering why I so badly want to qualify to be in there with them. Dealing with the shame of having been a staff-person, a professional in places like these, and how I am now feeling so far from that rooted solidness. Remembering how I thought I had it all figured out, only to now be back right where I thought I'd never be again. Feeling humiliation at wanting so badly to be confined with them, to have someone tell me what to do—when most of these people would do anything not to be struggling with their symptoms or locked behind secure steel portals.

Yet however much I want help, I don't really want to be in a general locked psych ward, which is what my future seems to be if I don't somehow convince the screening teams that I need a more specialized eating disorder program. So here I am. I don't know what else to do other than what I've done before, and I feel crazy. Starving has always led me back to myself, somehow, via treatment, via meal plans, via supervised eating, structured groups and intensive private sessions. Somehow this process, however fucked up it seems, has helped me find what I really am apart from this twisted frozen methodical pattern.

I take another triangle-sized piece of tortilla into my mouth and roll it around on my tongue. A minute goes by. I bite into the doughy, pasty glob, sucking the juices from the mass, extracting all the flavor I can out of it. It will be a while until I will allow myself to eat again. I've got to make it last.

32

CARL'S JR.

A twelve-year-old girl sits across the table from me, grimacing.

Her arms are crossed in protest over her prepubescent chest, and she's looking away from the plate in front of her. Around the table sit three other teenagers as well as a dietary aide. The aide is encouraging this young child to try to join in.

"You need to at least try, dear. I know you don't want to be here and that you think it's all an overreaction. You have to try..."

As she goes on, I remember my times as a staff person at the treatment center, trying to urge those rebellious teens to join me in eating a "normal" meal, and wish the aide all the luck in the world. I also wish myself all the luck in the world. What exactly am I doing back here in the patient seat?

In front of me is a "natural burger," a recent addition to the Carl's Jr. menu to try to entice the more health conscious to join their ranks of eaters. I have brought this meal to the table as my "challenge meal" and am preparing to eat it while the others stare and try to avoid their own challenges. The burger looks perfect, stacked and wrapped in its waxed paper cover. Next to the burger rests a "handful" of fries—the dietitian has guided me in choosing how many to equal a serving, and I have counted them out.

I pick up the burger and the wrapper crinkles in my grasp. As it nears my mouth, I can smell all of the deliciousness—toasted bread, pickles, medium-rare meat, ketchup—weaving aromas into my nostrils. I open my mouth and place the burger inside, taking a sizeable bite to prove that I am challenging myself enough. My teeth gnash through crisp lettuce, meat, tomatoes and sauce, and the entire glob congeals as I chew. Juices of many flavors trickle down my throat, and the collective taste of hamburger satiates my senses.

I put the burger down, picking up a napkin and wiping the sauce that has squirted out and marked my cheek as evidence. I chew, chew, and try not to show my anxiety to these others around the table. Somehow, I have made it my job to be the inspiration to these young eating disorder sufferers, and I've begun to wonder just who I'm doing this work for. It's all become jumbled, actually, ever since I made my way back here to treatment, but I am doing my best with the gift I have been given by the County Mental Health Department. It took a lot of convincing to get here, after all.

I see The Grimacer across the table, and remember the times when I'd pretended to hate food, when I pretended to rebel against "Them," when I wanted to be Someone With A Serious Problem. I remember being her. But I'd been sixteen, and it's kind of shocking to see this twelve year old girl walking down the same path.

Twelve. Twelve! What exactly is going on in our world where this is happening?

I look down and see my waiting fries. I pick up a few of them, resisting the impulse to split each fry in half; to eat one at a time, slowly. I shove the small handful into my mouth and chew the crisp, salty carbohydrate experience. I feel the others staring at me, wondering how I am showing such gluttony without protest or complete emotional breakdown. I close my eyes and savor, trying not to let their stares bore holes of doubt into me.

I want to get better. I worked hard to get here. I want to eat this burger. I want to love eating this burger. I want to honor this struggle and overcome it.

I open my eyes and see that The Grimacer has now turned the chair away from us and is staring off into the opposite wall. The aide has gotten up from the table and is preparing to call her parents if she doesn't comply.

I crinkle the wrapper between my fingers again as I bring the hamburger up to my mouth for another bite. I remember my writhing Dark Goddess inside. I am feeding Her. Even through Her screams, I will love Her.

I send out caring thoughts for the girl who may or may not survive the harrowing journey ahead of her. I eat my hamburger, and my fries, and try to show I am strong.

*T*hings took another turn.

This time, in treatment, in sharing her confusion, awareness and curiosity, she saw the clinicians encouraging her and asking to know more.

Hope entered again as she opened to the possibility that despite her struggle with this part of herself, she may still have something worthwhile to offer to others.

She suddenly understood that her ideas and wonderings might be powerful teachings, and that when shared could help others.

She suddenly understood it was her purpose to be in relationship with this intense force within her, to that which caused so much struggle with food and body, to give it, and her, the voice to speak.

33

THE KITCHEN WITCH MAKES BREAD

I am standing in front of the stove of my studio apartment.

The lights are dimmed, and there are candles lit around the stove's surface, flickering. Ethereal music dances through the air as I turn to the wall where my special apron hangs behind me. Before taking it off of its hook, I grasp both sides of the bottom half and spread it out to look at it. On this surface, I have hand-stitched a witch at her cauldron against a starlit black background.

I take a moment to admire this creation, although the skeptic in me has its moment to snicker. *You know this is all bullshit, don't you? Why are you putting effort into this nonsense?*

This is a familiar conversation. It used to really throw me, this skeptic, but recently I've become stronger in challenging this voice with my healthier self. Before it was just all a part of the tangled mess of my mind—now I'm learning to talk to my "parts" out loud. Hello crazy person!

My hands release the thick green material and it flops back against the wall, swaying slightly from its hook as I respond. "Well of course it could be bullshit, but despite this possibility I am doing it anyway. I am infusing my own chosen meaning into my relationship with food. Whether or not it is 'real' is not the point here. I appreciate your keeping me from getting kooky and fanatic about it, but your doubt will not hold me back from playing 'make believe,' if you will, anymore. Thanks for sharing."

Yeah...whatever. You've failed to help me see the purpose, but go ahead and waste your time.

"The purpose is to *play*. To experiment, to *do* something instead of sitting around frozen because nothing seems worth pursuing according to your rules of purpose. Again, I appreciate your keeping me in reality, but let's just take a moment to remember the time when I was a child and playing didn't have to have purpose—I just played. *We* just played. Can we just pretend that now? That we're *playing* here?"

Uh, hello, you're an adult, raVen...we're not children anymore and using our time is important. It should be used to work towards something significant—giving back to the community, etc. What purpose is dressing up and playing with your food in the kitchen going to serve in the world?

"I have two answers to that one! The first is that I don't know what purpose it has, meaning that it could have deeper purpose than what you and I can see right now. In the doing of this play, I may open up new worlds and ideas that I might not have just sitting here with you intellectually debating about meaning and angst. Or not. Maybe there's no meaning in it at all.

"The second answer is that just the purpose of playing is enough—enough to nourish that part of me that is so hammered by you to be a task master. Just some joy, just some whimsy, just some creativity...it's like a vitamin I need, and to make believe is to consume that vitamin."

Silly. You don't need play to survive, I think you should reconsider the word "vitamin" as it points to something that is essential to staying alive. Playing is extra. Playing is not really needed, just some fluff to make life seem pretty. I keep you focused on the essentials, like exactly what you need to eat to stay alive, like using your time to work and make a living, like making a major change in the world we live in.

"I hear you, I really do. And I think you're the perfect voice to keep that part of my life in line. But the part of my life that is about thriving, and enjoying and growing and creating...THAT is the part that needs another voice to support it. I don't expect it to be you, but I *will* bring that voice in to help me do this.

"I'm tired of life being so gray and flat, and this is the way I am choosing to explore infusing it with joy—an unnecessary but lovely nutrient. Feel free to come along with me and this other voice, but know that your direction won't be leading the conversation, okay? Let me know by all means if I am slacking on keeping myself fed or clothed or making the bucks! But geez...let me PLAY."

All right, well it's obvious I cannot talk any sense into you. I guess I will just be here for you when your play becomes unsatisfying and meaningless. I know you'll come back in despair like you always do. Play doesn't satisfy you, it hasn't since you were very little, and I know that. But try anyway, it's no skin off my back.

"All right, I *will* try. I think what I am exploring here is who exactly isn't satisfied with playing. Maybe it's *you*. Maybe it's some other part. All I know is I want to practice playing. Maybe by doing so, I will find out what part of me is disappointed and needs to run back to you and your gray, lifeless reality. I will be prepared to meet that part, thanks to your words, and when I do, I will go from there. Yet I will not let the possibility of despair or disappointment keep me from playing this time. Just this time. I'll see how it goes and then re-evaluate."

Fine, whatever. Have "fun."

I take a breath and come back into the moment, slightly shaken by the contact with this part of myself—the cold, hard, atheist, existential skeptic. I force myself to feel my bare feet on the linoleum floor and I close my eyes, breathing this breath. I tune into the dark, lilting notes of the music playing, and find myself swaying side to side, attuning to its rhythms.

I feel my body from the inside, my back, my arms and the slight tingling in my hands. I breathe in again, then release. Slowly I open my eyes, but only halfway, staring into the flicker of the golden glow of the burning candles surrounding the stove. I turn back around to the apron on the wall, and reach to lift it off of its hook. I smile as I carefully place the neck strap over my head until it rests at the back of my neck.

I smooth the fabric down the front of my body and grasp the straps at my sides, pulling them into a tie at my lower back. I turn to the stove again, and take in the sight of the bowls of herbs I've prepared, the open book of ritual, waiting, and the incense burner with its corresponding red lighter resting at its side.

I pick up the lighter and hold it under the tip of the incense until it catches fire. I watch the flame for a moment, like a child in awe for the first time, and then blow it out. The scent of copal infuses my nostrils as smoke curls up into the air like snakes. Something begins humming me. The ritual has begun.

I focus myself on the items in front of me. I grasp the open bag of flour and tip it over the shining silver bowl placed on the counter. Flour clouds poof up into the air as the powdery stream builds a mountain in the center of the bowl.

I put the bag down and hold the cold oval shape of an egg in my hand. I take a moment to thank the possible life for its sacrifice, and then break its shell over the glistening rim. As I pry open the broken shell, its slimy contents gloop out onto the top of the mountain.

Next, I look to a small crystal glass of liquid that sits on the counter near the bowl. Inside of it rests blood, collected from my recent menstruation. I think of all of the work I have done, and that this dear, dear, loyal body has done, to be menstruating again. It is astounding to me, and I breathe in and out gratitude. I bring the clear glass goblet into my hand and tip it slightly to allow for a few drops of thick crimson to sink into it all. Salt, sugar, water and yeast join this mass, and I hold my wooden spoon as I stir it all together.

Blessed be, these Cakes of Light. Blessed be, this Bread of Life. Blessed, blessed be.

I begin to feel resistance in my stirring, and put the spoon down. I dip my fingertips back into the open bag and gather some flour into my hands. I smooth the fine granules over my palms and immerse my fingers into the ball of dough. I begin to knead, infusing my intent into this matter. *May this be a conscious creation of goodness, nourishment and ease of digestion. May I channel this from mind to substance.*

Bread of life, water of life. I think of Inanna's helpers, feeding her cold, lifeless body these things. I look at my helper hands, making this for me, and soon, how they will feed me the bread and water of life, too.

The dough feels so delicious, sticky-sensual, pumping, squeezing, oozing through my fingers. I stretch the mass; I knead it. I appreciate it. I honor it. I then begin to pinch off bits and place them into slots in a greased muffin tin. I look over to see the heated coils of the toaster oven waiting for this alchemical vessel, and carry the tin to place it inside. The warmth envelops the tray as I slide it in. I look at this mystery, this potential, this self-created amazingness I have crafted with my will. I remember the fear of this substance, the avoidance, and how that is so very far from me today.

Bread of life, water of life. Two things I have restricted, now used to create. I gaze into the oven and wait for my nourishment to rise. The critical voice has left me.

*A*rmed with these new experiences, she found hope.

She found that maybe, just maybe, Spirit might possibly be at her back. She found herself able to embrace where she was as valuable and worthy, that even though she still struggled with food, she had something to offer.

Maybe, just maybe.

She was finally able to consider sharing with a wider audience, to come out from feeling shame or suspicion of people's projections about her journey.

Armed with new confidence in her journey simply as it was, she was finally able to begin writing her story in preparation to share it with the world.

34

SHRIMP

The hot sun warms my exposed shoulders, oozing in like honey.

Remember when those bones jutted out? I reflect on the shame I felt wearing tank tops in the not too-distant past. *Oh, the scrawny, sickly appearance I'd emanated. But now I'm recovered, whatever THAT means. I really HATE that word—why would I want to re-cover myself? Why not un-cover? Dis-cover? Re-member?*

The thoughts trail off as I snap back into the present, sunny, perfect day moment. It feels good to walk, to get my body moving, after a morning of feeling so heavy, stuck and weighted down beneath emotions. I breathe the fresh air and let myself be distracted by the reality of the world around me.

I feel my feet meeting the ground, one at a time. I listen to the sound of their cadence as I make my way down the boulevard to the store. I pass the local middle school, where there are lines of parents in shining parked cars waiting to pick up their rascally children. I detour around this happening, and a memory arises of my mother coming to retrieve me from school in the sputtering, rusty Pinto. She'd had on tattered, bleach-stained clothes and reeked of cigarette smoke. She'd always come that way, apparently just to embarrass me.

A bird passes before my eyes, just feet in front of me, singing. I re-tune my focus to follow this sound as I continue past the school and towards the market. I cross the boulevard and approach the store's entrance.

Six shrimp. One avocado. Salsa. One onion.
I repeat this in my head over and over as I enter the store, to keep my mind from exploding into anxious chaos. As always, I am hit by the

craziness of everything—the fifty-seven different kinds of chocolate bars to my left; the display of colors and mounds of produce, shining; the laughing clerks, the crying babies; the hundreds of smells congealing in my nose from the various hot bars and sampling stations; the people passing by. I anxiously make my way through this, head down, over to the seafood counter.

Six shrimp. One avocado. Salsa. One onion.

I approach the station, briny scents hitting my nostrils. The clerk is a burly, jovial, deep-voiced creature. *Oh man, this guy has a totally intense energy—it's hard to even look at him. Gah! I hope I can speak today.*

I brace myself, as these are often the ones who hit me like lightning.

Six shrinp, six shrimp, six shrimp. Just ask. Six shrimp.

"Well, hello there!" the jovial creature booms at me. "What goodness can I get for you today?"

Using all of my might to steady myself from the waves of his vibration, I pretend to be cool and ask, "Uh, yeah, can you tell me the source of these jumbo shrimp? Were they farmed or wild?" The man laughs, probably tired of being asked these questions repeatedly.

"Oh! Well, they've been raised with caring parents, an ethical education and a well-rounded diet...that's why they cost so much. Ha! Jumbo shrimp, the oxymoron!" Exclamations continue, with winking aimed at me sporadically. "How much can I get for ya?"

Shaking my head from his lifeness rattling me, I say, "Cool. Can I have six shrimp?"

I watch him stop for a few seconds, tuning into his energy as as I do with everything. In my head shouts a million different reasons why he hovers (*How could she only want six? That's ridiculousness! She must be single. Lonely. Or maybe she's ANOREXIC, the poor lass!*) but soon the moment of hesitation is over and he wraps up my six shrimp, giving me the tiny package. "There ya go...good day!" he says, nodding at me as he quickly moves to the next customer.

I breathe deeply and turn to face the vastness of aisles I must contend with to claim the rest of my "pleasurable variety" ingredients. The familiar overwhelm starts to rise in me, and my head starts to swim with confusion as well as a temptation to leave the store ASAP. Instead, I quickly start in with my focusing mantra:

Salsa. Salsa. Salsa. Salsa.

Condiments, good tastes, adding a little extra will help your life grow.

I keep repeating these words over and over until finally arriving at the salsas. I stand in front of the array. *Only about 40 different ones to choose from.* I snort, trying to use self-sarcasm to shake me from the impending freeze of anxiety.

Whilst reviewing them all, a woman behind me is talking at someone on her Smartphone: "Dearie, I *know* you don't want to do it, but it is *summer* after all! Time to cleanse and be my beautiful girl! Stop whining, you should be grateful I am willing to pay for it, I'm getting you the ingredients now and you'll start tomorrow. Yes I know....yes of course you don't want to do it...yes I know it seems like misery...but only for the first seven days! After that you'll feel so motivated! So light! And clear! I swear to you, dearie, trust me. You've been depressed and kind of lazing around, I know this will help. No, no, I don't want to hear it. I'll be home soon. Remember, your mother loves you!"

I always seem to either attract or tune into these ironic conversations. Is the universe taunting me or showing me the sad hilarity of the lifestyle I am trying my hardest to avoid? I shudder, thinking what it must be like to be on the other end of that phone, on the other end of that life. I am so perplexed at how people can do this and not fall down the slippery slope of destruction I always do when trying to "eat clean." Heaven forbid this daughter goes into that realm. I take a moment and offer a prayer, then face the wall of options once again.

Jalapeno pineapple, mild. Roasted pepper, spicy. Salsa Casera.

Glass. Aluminum. Isn't aluminum causing Alzheimer's or something?

20, 18, 12, 8, 4-ounce jar. Here we are again.

The mother whistles annoyingly behind me, choosing her maple syrup for its purity, no doubt. I've been staring at the shelf for ten minutes, I'm now surpassing the obsession of the mother behind me.

For god's SAKE, just PICK one. It's just salsa. It's just salsa. It's just salsa.

I hear the mother walk away, heels clicking on the runway. I spend a few more minutes coming to the conclusion that price and a small size for my one culinary adventure will be the choice point.

A four ounce can of Salsa Casera clunks into my almost empty basket, rolling and threatening the delicate shrimp. I plod on towards the produce buffet. On my way, I detour down the pharmacy aisle to look at the Ensure stacked medicinally on the shelf. I like to stand and look at rows and rows of Ensure for some reason. I never buy, I just stare. I do this often.

I stand here again before this odd glory and remember when that was all I wanted to drink, so simple. The only choices: vanilla, chocolate, strawberry.

I begin another mantra to re-focus myself:

Avocado. Onion. Avocado. Onion. Avocado. Onion.

I depart from the the sweet and creamy six-packs and make my way to the mounds of produce. I stare at all of these fresh items, at the way the water droplets rest on leaves and in crevices. I feel the freeze coming on again, as if hypnotized by colors and shapes and the repeating cycle of overhead misting.

I come back to self-consciousness.

Just choose one of each. One avocado. One onion.

I urge myself to the relevant area and plop one of each in my basket.

Weirdo. You're such a weirdo!

I make my way to the checkout counter. There are two people ahead of me. I close my eyes and breathe again, calming myself. I look to my left and see the shelves of items meant to facilitate last-minute purchases.

But no! Before you can check the hell out of here, you must face the absurdness of…the magazine rack!

Make this delicious calorie-laden meal! reads one corner of a magazine cover. *Try our liquid cacao fast!* reads the opposing corner. What an amazing conflict of twisted human desire.

Angelina Jolie is Anorexic! The horror! a tabloid magazine proclaims. *Paleo dinners that fill you up, don't leave you hungry—but help you lose weight anyway! Decrease inflammatory foods! Eat more low-glycemic vegetables!*

Blah blah blah blah. Blah, blah blah blah. Can't we please make it stop?

I am now next in line. I pull my wad of various cards and scraps of paper from my pocket, searching for my food stamp card. I take it out of its cover and look at the cashier, judging how she'll view me. What will she think of me, a white, capable, seemingly put-together female, using a food stamp card? I've gone back and forth about this guilt hundreds of times before in my mind, sometimes choosing my checker purposely to avoid having to feel too much guilt or shame. Sometimes I realize that I am fine just the way I am, and that, for a time, this is what is needed. Yet the check stand always tests that theory.

Finally I meet the eyes of the checker and feel waves of intensity. I can sense her expectation of a cheery interaction.

"Hello! Oh, shrimp, eh? They're so good, all grilled up with sauces…I guess it's worth it to veer into cholesterol land sometimes, huh?" She smiles at me, apparently having a conversation with herself, rambling and high on caffeine.

If there were only words to describe to this woman what I really think.

"Having a good day, ma'am….ahem?" She has realized there is another in this reality.

"Yeah," I say. "I'm having a day, thanks."

The checker's face is deadpan as she realizes I'm not going to be cheery with her.

"Well. There's your receipt, ma'am," the checker says, a slight ire in her voice.

I nod and put my stuff in my canvas bag and move out of line, out into the brightness of blue sky once again. I let out a sigh of relief.

At least THAT'S over. Now I only have to deal with cooking it, with the roommates' hovering chaotic energy. Ugh. Why am I doing this again? I'm already nauseous. But I will do it. Because I am privileged to have this money, this time, a home to cook this food. I am privileged to be alive, after battling with this obsession for so many years. I will do it to feed the Kitchen Witch that wants to live through me, one that wants to enjoy food, life, a little magic. This is one step to get there.

I stop for a moment. Something in me is judging this placating, positive voice.

Why do you always encourage yourself with this statement, even though a large part of you feels it's bullshit? Even though you're still here, being weird and struggling with this after all these years?

Ah, the familiar critic...I've had so many internal conversations with it, convincing it to not convince me to end it all.

I HAVE to do it. Over and over. This is the only way I can get through. I know you don't believe in the use of pleasure, of eating more than what's necessary, or that there's any joy that can be experienced in life. Only overwhelm, only pain, only heaviness...I know. Evidence strongly supports your viewpoint, looking at the life I've led. I value you, keeping me focused on what's important, on survival, in this psychically intense body and world. But I want more and I will continue trying, for as long as I can. I'm not sure WHY I keep trying, but I want MORE.

The critic is silent for some reason. I look up at the sun and shift the bag on my shoulder for comfort. I hope the shrimp isn't decimated by now, squished in its little package and canceling out all of what I just went through to get it. We'll see.

I take in another deep breath and head home.

35

THE DAILY SALAD

I am standing at the kitchen counter.

In front of me is a cutting board, a knife, and a bag of various salad ingredients. To the right of the cutting board rests a 1/4 cup measuring container, a tablespoon, and my salad bowl. I look up, away from the cutting board and out the front window.

The sun is shining brightly on freshly watered grass. The landlord lugs the compost with his sweaty arms across my field of vision, and his perky puppy prances after him to investigate what the activity is all about. I see my new car shining in the driveway, and upper middle class white neighbors strolling down the street on their daily walk with their manicured dogs. I look back to my cutting board. I feel a twisted sense of gratitude and emptiness as I contemplate my place in the world.

I begin my lunchtime measuring ritual. First, I lift the leftover salmon from the bag and the glass that contains it is cold to my touch. I set the container down gently to prevent it from making too much noise. I peel away the red plastic lid and lean into the bowl to sniff the contents to make sure they are still good. They pass.

I pick up the measuring cup; its silver surface catches the sunlight and flashes into my eyes as I dip it into the shredded salmon. I scoop the cup full, then pick up a fork and tamp the salmon down, filling and primping until I see that the top is perfectly flat and exactly 1/4 cup. I dump the contents into the waiting salad bowl.

I listen for others in the house. It seems silent, but my roomates could come up at any time. I pivot, turning abruptly to the sink. I run the measuring cup under the water and shake it dry, shoving it into the drawer quickly so no one will see that I've measured my food. I turn back to the cutting board.

I take out the next storage bowl and peel away the lid to reveal a freshly cut avocado half. I grasp it gently, feeling its pimpled thick skin, and place it on the cutting board. I slide out a knife from its wooden block and hold it in my right hand, placing it against the dark skin. The ridges of the knife's surface slide through the buttery green flesh and the avocado splays out into two quarter slices. I pick one slice up and use the knife to dice the soft fruit, watching as the chunks drops into the bowl. I put the other slice away for tomorrow.

Next, I lift the sauerkraut out of the bag and set it on the counter. I open the bag and out rushes a briny odor, with slight hints of caraway. I pick up the metal tablespoon at my side and dip it into the bag, again fussing with it until its surface is flat, perfect. I empty this into the bowl.

I pivot around and glance at the clock on the stove. It is now 11:45am. Only fifteen minutes to wait until it is time to eat.

I turn back around and pick up a stainless-steel pot from the pile of drying dishes on the counter, setting it up right in front of me on the wood surface. I lift out a bag of pre-cut, washed kale, a carrot, and a jar of bone broth, setting them down in a row. A perfect row. I look at them for a moment, appreciating the lines and colors, how they almost look like art, highlighted by the beam of sunshine coming in the window. I hesitate so as not to disturb this beauty, and then judgments come rolling in:

Look at you! Measuring again! After all that work you did in treatment...you did it there, why not here? Why do you have such a hard time just making a meal? How many years will it take? How many more dietitians, how many treatment programs will you have to go through? Hopeless! You're just broken, you've shriveled up your natural eater and blown it away!

I soothe myself with compassionate thoughts and try not to fall prey to the exclamations. I will measure if it makes it safe for me to eat what I need. Until I can do differently.

I focus back onto my task, and open the waiting jar of bone broth. I unscrew the metal lid, set the lid down, and hold the jar up to the light to read the measurements on the side of the jar. I need to pour until it reaches twelve ounces, so my pour is delicate. A steep angle could release way more and I need for it to be right. I watch the gloopy gelatinous liquid trickle into the pot, pouring and lifting to check the jar a few times. It reaches the line so I put the jar down and seal it. Next I open the kale bag and pour a large amount into the pot on top of the liquid. I laugh as I "let loose" with the kale, allowing myself to not measure it. How has my life come to this, where this feels freeing?

I ponder my appreciation for perfection, a measured life, while also feeling the struggle of my inner adventurous tomboy—restrained and bucking in the reins I have him tied down with. I don't know how to let him live, so I don't let myself think about him or his frustration for too long. I have learned to ignore his clawing to get out. I resume.

The carrot is now in my hand. I feel its coldness, its hairy ridges, as I hold it down to the cutting board. The knife slices through the orange root, making one, two, three, four, five slices. I put the knife down and gather up the slices and plop them into the pot. Now the greens and oranges and silvers are dancing together. I take the pot to the stove and turn the heat on low to steam the contents.

The clock says 11:52 am.

I put the lid on the pot and remember I need to toast the bread so that it will be done at the same time as the steaming. I go to the freezer and pull out the drawer, packed full with my roommates' various delicious items. Only my bread and frozen bananas make room for themselves there.

I open the sealed bag and grab out a previously measured chunk of whole wheat bread and reseal the bag. Its icy edges poke at my hand as I use my other hand to slide the freezer shut. I make my way to the toaster oven and set the bread onto the toast rack. I close the door and turn the timing knob to a dark toast, to revive and crisp the bread from its frozen state.

I hear someone coming, so I walk briskly to the counter where my supplies are, throwing the tablespoon into the sink and rearranging my things so I don't look like an OCD crazy person. My roommate walks through the kitchen and says hello, I say hello back. Luckily, she's not stopping to actually connect because it would be really inconvenient right now…she might see me. I take note that she's going to the laundry room, and that she'll probably be back through shortly. I turn to the cutting board and plot how I can finish so as not to look weird when she comes back through.

I look at what I have left to measure and see I am done—or would have been in the past. I remember the commitment I made to my dietitian and calculate the calories in my head to see where I am: 80+100+20+90+30=320. Damn. I know I promised I would get to 400 but feel the familiar struggle rise in me not to do so. I feel my head start to rumble with fighting gods and choices of what to add and what it might feel like to eat more and whether there will be pain and discomfort and when I might be hungry again if this makes me too full.

I am tempted, very tempted to not add anything, to stop the war in my head from plaguing me, very tempted to align with the voice inside that says that 80 calories doesn't really matter. Yet I find myself somehow in the midst of this storm walking over to the cupboard and pulling out a packet of hemp seeds. I turn the packet over and see that one tablespoon equals about sixty calories. I decide sixty calories is better than no extra at all and feel myself walking back over to the counter, pulling the tablespoon out of the sink and pouring hemp seeds into its concavity. I look around for my roommate and hear she is still fussing with the laundry machine, or folding or whatever. I look back to the tablespoon in my hand, lift it up to eye level to check the amount just in case, and dump it quickly into the bowl. I rinse the tablespoon, shake it off, and shove it into the drawer.

The pot lid is rumbling, steam spurting out, and I rush over to the stove to turn off the heat. My roommate comes walking back through the kitchen, her face partially hidden behind an overflowing basket of clothes. She moves past me to and through the door back to her room, saying nothing. I sigh with relief.

The clock now reads 12pm. I have made it, and will actually be eating later than lunchtime. Some part of me registers this as exhibiting a sense of extra restraint. I feel a jumbled sense of pride, and shame, at this thought.

I go over to the cupboard and pick out my favorite drinking cup. I bring it to the side of the stove and set it down. I pick up the pot and just slightly fidget the lid so there is a little room for the broth to filter out into the cup. I tip the pot over the cup and watch the now liquefied substance stream slowly into the cup. Hot vapors rise from its surface.

I bring the pot and the remainder of its strained steamy contents over to my salad bowl. It has been waiting for me in the sun. I remove the pot's lid and tip the contents into the bowl. I wash the pot, shaking it dry and put it away into the cupboard. I put all of the contents I have splayed out on the counter back into the bag—the glass bowls first, then the bone broth jar, and finally the bags of veggies. I wash the cutting board and the knife, returning them to their places so that there is no evidence that I have prepared anything or have even been here. This seems to make me feel less anxious. I go to the toaster oven and remove the perfectly golden bread cube, then walk it over to my bowl and place it on top of the salad.

I lift the full salad-fixings bag and put it on my shelf in the fridge, closing the door on another day's ritual. I prepare to consume this meal, like I have hundreds of times: alone, safe in my room behind closed doors, in front of Netflix, savoring this carefully created meal bite by bite over the course of an hour. I hope it won't give my stomach any trouble. It hasn't most times, but today I added sixty calories of hemp seeds, so who knows what might happen. I snicker darkly as I think of this being the only remnants of a sense of adventure, of danger, in my life as I know it.

Holding the bowl and cup of broth, I ascend the staircase to my safe place. I arrive at the top of the stairs and look to my left, through and into my roommate's room. The perky puppy is lying there now, all four legs in the air, and her eyes are staring directly into mine. The sun's rays stream in from the window onto the bed, highlighting the soft fur belly of this creature. A wave of love hits me and I look down at my bowl, my perfectness. For a minute I want to set it down and sit with the dog for some play. Instead, I tell her I love her and then turn away.

I open my door and see the seat I sit in so many hours and days of my life, eating this same controlled meal. I sigh, and am aware of the nagging in me that says I may be "healthy," I may be menstruating, but that this is not what I really want. There are so many voices. I breathe in again and close the door behind me, shutting the portal to that sun-soaked love creature. I shuffle over to my chair and sit down. I turn on the computer and begin the meal, like I have so many times before.

I want this to be different, but I don't know how to get there. Where is "there" anyway? I remember that doctor, so long ago saying, "Just eat a burger and fries, little lady," and wishing it was that easy. Is it?

Netflix has uploaded and I press play. I sip the savory broth and begin the eating portion of my ritual again, losing myself in the same flavors, the same textures, the same safe measurements, the digital storyteller, and the mini-series characters I've grown "close" to. I forget the voice inside that wants so much more.

36

TURKISH COFFEE

I'm standing in front of a propane stove.

A handcrafted metal counter has been tailored to nestle it into an indentation, all made specifically to fit California food vending code purposes. The surrounding walls have been salvaged from mobile home demolitions—they are a fake woody brown, and the grain patterns on them are mismatched. Strings of white Christmas lights hang around the edges of the bow-top ceiling, their soft glow bringing warmth to the interior, and also to me on this drizzly evening.

The serving window is open, looking out onto the freshly moistened dark pavement. A black glittering curtain hangs down over the window, and a person sits waiting at the cafe table placed just outside. I am preparing a cup of Turkish coffee for this customer, one of the popular items I offer from my handmade bohemian caravan food cart.

I light the propane stove and it comes to life with blue-green gaseous flames. I pick up the long-handled copper *ibrik* from the counter to my right, a shiny gift purchased by a dear friend during her travels to Turkey. I hold the *ibrik* under the faucet and fill it about halfway with water, then place it on the stove's metal surface. Flames dance around the copper base, as if glad to have a partner to engage with. While the water comes to a boil, I pick up the container that holds freshly ground Turkish coffee, and unscrew the top. A whoosh of bright aroma hits my nose, and I pause to breathe in this coveted scent. Into the fine grounds, I have added cardamom and the odors swirl together in the air. I scoop one and one half teaspoons into the *ibrik*, so that the finely-ground mixture floats on the water's surface. And now the wait begins.

For some reason, I feel the fabric of the skirt I am wearing brush against my legs. I look down and notice its complicated patterns, of magentas and oranges and purples. A black lacy shawl rests over my shoulders, its fringed edges dangling over the top of the skirt. I wonder what my child-like self would think of me now—from tomboy to this!

The scent of coffee pulls me back to my task at hand. The grounds have now spread out into a moistened brown layer on top of the water, and small iridescent bubbles are forming around its edges. I watch, waiting for the right moment to remove the *ibrik* from the heat to prevent the concoction from boiling over. I grasp the handle and pull it away from the stove, letting the bubbles come to a rest. After a few seconds, I place the *ibrik* back on the flame again, repeating the process of bringing the solution to its peak temperature, then removing. I do this for a total of three times. I love that this ritual is practiced culturally, because following its steps soothes me.

On the same counter at my right sits a demitasse ceramic cup. I take the *ibrik* and hold it at an angle over the cup, pouring ever-so-slowly. The dark liquid flows in a single stream and leaves a caramel-colored crema floating at its surface. Steam rises from the hot, aromatic brew and I lean down to take in the scents.

I pour an additional cup for myself, and bring the other to the window.

"Your coffee is ready."

The customer rises and comes to the window. On the counter before him I have several tarot decks set out for people to play with while waiting. The Fool card stares at him as we complete our transaction.

"Thank you." He takes the demitasse into his hands, cradling it, and brings it to his nose. "Ahhhh. I miss this smell! It reminds me of my travels to Europe so many years ago. And the warmth of this cup, it's a good thing on a rainy evening like this."

"I'm curious to know your experience of the flavors, since you've consumed this coffee in its traditional countries. I spent some time trying to study 'authentic' recipes with different Turkish coffee purveyors, but every one of them was different! I finally settled on this one."

A moment rests between us as we both bring our cup's rim to our lips. The intensity of the bitter, slightly acidic brew bursts onto my taste buds; the resinous fragrance of the cardamom also dancing there. I close my eyes and savor this delectable brew, breathing deeply.

"Ahh! This is delightful! The tastes are similar to what I experienced in my travels, however I'm not tasting something…rosewater, maybe? Some of the cafes had it in their coffees, some didn't. Did you use rosewater?"

Lost in my reverie, I take a moment to respond. I open my eyes slowly.

"No, but I thought of it. I'm glad you're enjoying it. I am too. Would you like a piece of dark chocolate to accompany it? This is my favorite combination."

I unfold the gold wrapping of a bar of chocolate resting next to the tarot deck. I feel its silky surface between my fingers and apply pressure to break it into a chunk for us to share.

"Thank you. I've never tried this combo before."

He takes the chocolate into his mouth and bites through the bar's surface with his teeth. A faint chopping sound comes from this movement. I watch as he brings the cup back up to his lips and tilts it to deliver more of the dark brew.

I take the chocolate similarly into my mouth, but have chosen a smaller chunk so that no biting is required. I let the chunk rest on my tongue, awaiting its slow dissolution. Rivulets of sweet bitterness begin to stream across my tongue, coating my cheeks. I bring the cup to my mouth and take a small sip. The spices, aroma and milky sweetness swirl and rise to my head, to that sacred gustatory system that allows me this pleasure, this divine experience.

I open my eyes to see this customer in his own enjoyment experience. "Ahhh! Such a great combination. I am inspired to carry on this tradition at home. I'm going to sit down and enjoy."

"If you'd like, take a card and read about it while you savor."

I shuffle the deck and lay it out for him to choose. He selects one and turns it over. I cannot see what he has chosen. He takes the description book and his card and tucks the book under his arm. He balances the demitasse and its saucer in his other hand and moves to sit at the table.

I take in the soft glow highlighting the contour of his face. I wonder about his travels, where he has been—yet another mysterious customer emerging from the crowd of this witchy festival I have been hired for. Across the pavement, there is a spotlight beaming out from a temple building dedicated to the goddess Isis. I look back to the man, the large umbrella shields him from the gentle drizzle. It brings me joy to see this scene: the handcrafted cart I am in, the steam rising from my customer's cup, and his quiet enjoyment of what I have created.

I stare down into the surface of the black liquid that remains in my cup and I can see the reflection of the overhead lights sparkling in it. As I gaze deeper, the surface becomes a pitch-black sky with stars. I imagine a raven flying through, cawing, and winking, at me. Somehow, despite my struggles with life, religion, my body, the back and forth of measuring, all of it... this magic winks back at me.

I take a slow breath in, feeling a deep sense of peace. I am so very grateful to be here.

37

VANILLA ICE CREAM, DEUX

I emerge from the Rite Aid through the whoosh of the mechanized doors.

I am propelled forward by air cooling and out into the searing heat of the California summer. In my hand is a vanilla ice cream cone, I can feel the subtle ridges of the cone imprinting my palm as I grasp it lightly.

Dribbles of liquefying ice cream are beginning to make their way down the sides of the scoop. I move in quickly with my waiting mouth to catch them before they wet the tops of my fingers rimming the cone's circumference. My tongue hits the icy cream and catches the first rivulets of milky sweetness. I lick upstream to the top and then dart to catch the next cascading dribble. I do this until the scoop appears solid and able to handle a moment of savoring the flavors. My eyes close. I am enjoying.

I hear the honk of a car going by, a man whistling. I can feel the squirmy energy arise in me, the discomfort and the realization that I am out here, on a corner of a busy intersection, licking a melting ice cream cone in delight, my tongue waving its flag of freedom to pleasure itself. I am terrified to open my eyes and face the possibility of gawking, creepy-smiling perverted humans driving by.

My stomach turns with nausea, and I am tempted to stop what I have come here intently to do. Subterranean voices start berating me:

Stop enjoying!
Stop the challenge!
Stop pushing yourself to allow for pleasure!
Dangerous!
What will they think of you?
Asking for trouble!

I know where some of these voices come from, but some intrude from unknown, perhaps ancestral, sources. It takes all of me to both turn the chatter down and summon up the courage to crack my eyelids slightly to see what is outside. I can feel the melting liquid dripping down over the edge of my handhold. I do not care. My breath has become shallow—I notice it and consciously make an effort to take a long slow inhale to calm myself.

Through my eyelashes, I see a red stoplight. I have positioned my head to look upwards first so I won't have to immediately look at THEM. I hear car engines rumbling, waiting. There are no whistles now, no catcalls. The smell of rubber and pavement snakes into my nostrils. I hear the sound of a crow, *caw-caw-cawing* on the telephone line above me. A slight warm breeze blows stray hairs across my face.

The crow has given me strength for some reason, an animal guide I suppose, urging me on, and I decide to open my eyes fully. I look down at the ice cream. It is in bad shape now, and I am conflicted whether to save it quickly with my mouth or to turn the cone over and let it plop to the sidewalk, releasing its rivulets to dance upon a new surface. The crow *caw-caw-caws* again. I decide to let it mean I need to swoop in and rescue the collapsing mass.

My neck cranes forward and my whole mouth encompasses what's left of the solid part of the scoop. My lips press together, capturing the deliciousness safely inside. The cold hits my brain all at once, tongue both bracing and enjoying this barrage of sensation. I have closed my eyes again, afraid of what or who is watching me, what it may cause them to do, whether I am safe. Voices of ecstasy collide with those of defense and fear and create a maelstrom in my head and gut.

Caw-caw-caw, goes the crow. I force my eyes to peel open again.

I take a breath and look up. I breathe out. There are cars whizzing by, none of them concerned with my microcosmic experience. I take another big breath in and send the out breath down through my body, out through the soles of my feet.

Grow grow grow, like roots into the earth, I chant to myself.

I adjust my posture, noticing I have hunched over slightly during this intensity. I feel my backbone stacking up straight, crown of my head reaching to the sky. I take another deep breath in and look down at my poor, soggy cone. The rest of the ice cream has become a pool of liquid in the base of the cone, I can feel the paper holding its edges starting to soften, bulging. I breathe in deeply, and then slowly let it out in a sigh—which suddenly becomes a laugh. I laugh, laugh, laugh, and nod my head, side to side, back and forth.

Caw-caw-caw! I look up to this crow conspirator and lift my cone to it, as if to toast its support in this hilarious travesty. With my head tilted skyward, I tip the rest of the cone's contents into my mouth and let the melted cream run like silk down my throat. I feel it creating a numbing ice river over the middle of my tongue on its way down.

A horn blares loudly as I do this, but there is no catcall, no hooting or hollering. I don't know if it is directed at me or just a useless rageful expression, but somehow, I don't care. My eyes are open, and I'm looking directly at the crow.

I can see the shimmering of its black blue purple green feathers now, glistening in the sunlight. It fidgets, as if it can feel my gaze. Waddle waddle waddle, it moves sideways along the tight electric line. Feathers ruffle, and its beak dives to nervously preen crevices.

The crow doesn't seem to like all of the attention. It lets out a squawk, and flies away for cover.

38

THE EGG SALAD SANDWICH

2017. Forty three years old.

It is dark, sitting here in the underground parking garage outside the ER.

Beside me sits an egg-salad sandwich. I've just effortlessly purchased it at the hospital cafeteria while waiting for my mother to get treatment. Uncharacteristically, there was no tormented, indecisive thinking about what to choose or any measuring involved in this purchase. I simply knew I'd enjoyed pre-packaged egg-salad sandwiches before, so this seemed like a good-tasting and sustaining choice.

Such a strange feeling to be a visitor at a hospital, after all the years I've spent living in them. Somehow, buying this sandwich in the cafeteria without giving it much thought felt like a victory. Especially because I spent the last four or so hours in and out of my mother's assigned ER room, listening to her moan and grieve over her malfunctioning, horrible body. Helping her put on adult diapers, fending off her temper aimed at—but not meant for—me.

In past years, I would've totally used this as an excuse to focus on controlling my food. Yet there I was, keeping my center as I shadowed her to the X-ray room, where the technician scanned her abdomen for yet another of her infamous blockages. My mother has been here so many times in the last ten years that the staff know her by name, like Cheers.

"I just can't get it out of me," I remember her saying, "and they never seem to find a goddamned thing...incompetent assholes! They think I'm crazy and I think they're asshole useless doctors!" I remember looking up at the technician, slightly embarrassed. He smiled at me and said nothing.

I've come to the car to rest, here in the silence. Mother's energy, her words, are like daggers, arrows, and sometimes black holes, sucking all the life out of me. So, I've learned to take breaks, set boundaries, when I'm called to attend to her. I love her, I really do, but it's exhausting.

I look up and see her hobbling out of the ER doorway. The security guard thinks she's some cute old lady and gives her a hand—he has no idea! My daughterly instinct compels me to get out of the car and go to her, leaving my egg-salad sandwich resting on the dashboard.

I walk across the parking lot and hold her arm, so withering and birdlike. She blasts out obscenities about the asshole doctors and their uselessness. I interrupt her, look into her eyes, and tell her I love her. She looks back at me, like she always does when I get present with her, eyes smiling, and her voice turns warm. She starts her course of gratitude for me, reminding me of how good I am to her, how horrible it must be to go through this with her. I stay silent and squeeze her hand.

We get to the car, I open the door for her. She plops her bird-like body into the passenger seat and I continue around the car to the driver's side and get in. My egg-salad sandwich is sitting there on the dashboard, and my mother is requesting we drive back home immediately, stating she's "so sick of being in this place again." I interrupt my mother and tell her I need to take a break and eat something first. She says, "Of course," like she understands.

I take the sandwich off of the dashboard, rip open the plastic sanitized package, and lift out a half. The bread is white, billowy. There are no vegetables lining the inside, just a gob of eggness, waiting to ooze out into my mouth as I bite. I enjoy the textures as they enter through my lips, chewing and savoring. Mom is sitting there beside me like she doesn't care. It's normal, this solitary experience: me eating, her sitting there abstaining. Yet out of nowhere, I am moved to offer her the other half of my sandwich. I expect her traditional refusal; I am already planning for it. *I'll save the other half for later—a snack.*

My mother, however, says yes, and I am surprised. As I give her the other half, a chunk of egg plops onto the gray plastic separating our seats. She takes the sandwich from me and starts eating it, somewhat ravenously, and I sit back, looking straight ahead so as not to stare, a bit stunned. I quickly resume my eating, savoring my half, bite by bite, sneaking nervous glances at her from the side of my field of vision. There is no discussion of how we never really eat together. The moment is being treated, wordlessly, like a normal, shared meal. But it isn't. I haven't ever had this experience. I've been with her as she pushes food around the plate to placate others' judgments about her, but never have I been next to her actually eating a meal. We sit in silence, I've no idea if she feels the weight of the floating tension like I do.

Both of us finish eating, and I decide that it's time to go. I pull out of the parking space and head up the ramp into the light above ground for the short drive home. We're laughing, and something's different.

We arrive at her home and I get out of the car. I go around and open the door for her. She grunts as she lifts herself up out of the seat. I take hold of her arm gently as we climb the stairs to her second-story apartment. Arriving at her door, there are flowers, some real and some fake, in pots all around the threshold. She jiggles her key into the door's lock and opens it, shuffling herself inside. I stay at the door and watch her, so fragile, moving away from me into the living room.

She turns around and shuffles back to me and looks me in the eyes, then pulls me close into her arms. There still is an A-frame gap between the lower parts of our bodies, that hasn't changed. She scratches my back with her long creepy fingernails as she grasps me.

"Love you," she says.

"Love you too, Ma. I better get going."

I walk away and see my mother standing at the door doing her weird wave thing at me, smiling. I get in my car and prepare for the long drive home.

This is the last time I will see my mother alive.

EPILOGUE

ON FULLNESS

About a year after my mother's death, I contracted yet another strange, un-diagnosable stomach illness, in which everything I ate was unable to be absorbed, passing its way violently through me. This went on for three straight weeks, and during this time I tried my hardest to keep up with the measured meal plan that had been successfully maintaining my weight since being in day treatment a few years back.

I pushed and tried to eat it all, but at some point my body just physically rejected every bit of it. I was terrified—letting go of this plan and trusting my body to guide me had had horrible consequences in the past. But I literally couldn't eat what I'd been eating anymore, it just passed right through. I scrambled, trying to meet my caloric needs by drinking the highest calorie clear liquids and bland foods, but none of it helped keep my hard-earned weight on. I decided to surrender, pushing when I could, and allowing for what my body couldn't accept, not knowing where it would take me.

On the fourth week, the diarrhea wasn't stopping. Again, I was petrified of what was happening to my body, afraid my heart would stop from loss of electrolytes. I brought myself into the ER, where they found me extremely dehydrated but ultimately couldn't really tell what was causing the trouble. No parasites or bacteria, just an extremely irritated digestive tract and a slight urinary tract infection—nothing that would warrant the extreme symptoms I was having. I was prescribed antibiotics, and although this also made me fearful, I hoped it would solve whatever was happening so I could just eat again. Fortunately, it did.

Yet there I was having lost pretty much all of the weight I had desperately fought my way into treatment to gain. For the first few days I was determined—I had a weight gain meal plan to follow, and I tried. I took myself out for hamburgers and fries, ice cream. And once again I was stopped by the fullness—the incredibly uncomfortable, almost PTSD-like reaction I have to my stomach being "overly" full.

Cramping, nausea, and panic took me over each time I pushed a meal and had to sit with this unexplainable terror. In treatment, I had others around, groups to keep me busy, therapists to talk about things while pushing up against this fullness. But in hindsight, we never really talked about this terror, this fullness and how its avoidance ruled me; we only discussed how to push through, how to distract myself until it passed.

Regardless, I wasn't in treatment anymore, and was without a safe structure to help me deal with this. There I was, stomach once again shrunken and appetite reduced, and alone. I looked to eating disorder support groups to help me. They only saw my "relapse" and that the eating disorder voice was winning, but that wasn't my experience at all.

It wasn't a critical voice. Rather, it seemed to be my *body*, screaming back at me, rejecting the food. Again, I felt like a stranger in a strange land. No support groups felt helpful, they only seemed to aim at pinning me into a box that I couldn't relate to.

The only solace I had was of the BodySoul work of Marion Woodman, which pointed at un-diagnosable symptoms in the body as being windows into healing. I leaned heavily into her writings, and found great kinship among others who resonated with her work.

Questions loomed once again in my mind about my body, my eating, my sanity. What was it that consistently went against my aims to maintain a strong, nourished self? There was no "eating disorder voice," no judgment of my weight, no wanting people to like me for being thinner. None of this consciously seemed to throw a wrench in my attempts at wellness. It simply seemed that over and over again, after a while of being nourished, my body rebelled, and had to bring me back to the liminal state of health where I'd teetered for most of my life.

I was perplexed, felt defeated, and wasn't quite sure what to do. I ate enough to maintain this lower weight, but again just enough so I wouldn't have to feel the pain, discomfort, and inexplicable terror of "too much" food. I felt angry, and wondered if it was worth it to push my way past all of this to only find myself here again.

Was I meant to stay here, in my small little cage, forever? I knew it might be possible that this was true, but again, the trooper in me had to keep going. Something in me had to put in every effort to truly see clearly about all of this. I was going to die someday, maybe someday soon. I wanted to know that I gave it my all to try to figure out what the hell my body was attempting to tell me, and what it wanted me to do.

So. I accepted my possible fate. I also kept eating what I could. I pushed it when I felt courageous enough to face the pain, and let myself not push when I felt scared. I sent love to my body. I watched what calmed it and what sent it into flight mode. I allowed myself to live in the complexity of the fact that what I was experiencing might be my eating "disorder," but that it might be something else entirely.

In being with myself, deeply, I've noticed patterns. At some point, I began to see that these patterns were ones I had been circling my entire life. I began to see that my whole existence, since I was a child, had been planned, designed, and measured to avoid The Fullness. I saw that not only did I organize everything around not feeling full of food, but also of not feeling full of relationships, other people's energies, responsibilities, creativity, and sexuality.

I began to see that something in me was incredibly uncomfortable with "too much" in general, and had devised ways to limit the amount of stimulation, demands and choices in my life. I validated that part of this was me being extremely sensitive to the energies and agendas and cultural brainwashing I was immersed in. I also started becoming curious about what it was, in my own body, that might be able to tell me more about its pain if I were to engage with it directly.

I began to see that feeling full, alive, and connected to others had become the trigger for immense trauma responses in my body, and I didn't see a real reason why. All I could see was that what made most people feel safe, encouraged and held, for some reason caused terror in me. So, I made it my goal to explore this reaction, to incoming Life itself, and to the astounding lengths I had taken to keep it siphoned to a trickle for so many years.

This is where I stand and continue to actively explore. So far, I have found the voice of a small child in the center of this terror. She reminds me of the meals she was fed by a mother who cooked while cursing the horrible life she lived. She reminds me of what it felt like to take that despair and rage into her stomach, into her little body and being expected to process and hold it within. She reminds me of the ghosts she felt in that house, and in her body. She reminds me of how much she hated this, how it all pulsed and scratched and pushed inside of her. She reminds me of how she could not stop it from happening, until of course, she found a way.

I am grateful that she is beginning to share herself with me. I know we have a lot of work to do.

In the end, she wrote her story.

In the end, she shared it with you.

In the end, it didn't matter whether she was symptom-free, or what the larger system thought, or that she seemed to be returning to old patterns.

In the end, she felt like she was beginning to see the spiral, the labyrinth, of her own soul's journey.

In the end, she felt, deep in her bones, that her struggles with food were way older than her, and that it may be a complex path to unravel her ancestors' traumas from her own.

In the end, she felt satisfied when she realized that she was a sacred being on a sacred journey, doing this sacred work.

*And in the end,
she knew
that this was just
the beginning.*

POSTSCRIPT

WHAT'S THE POINT?

This collection of memories was crafted to relay, at least in my experience, how my journey with depression and an "eating disorder" is NOT about body image, or about wanting to be skinny to be liked. While things seemed to have started out that way, I have found that my eating disorder is not about calories, about being misled by fashion magazines, about vanity or any of the things you see in "normal" mainstream media where these disorders are mentioned.

For me, this experience has been about going on a journey through light and shadow, to heal and re-member parts of myself. What it *has* been about is akin to a rite of passage, where the desire to not eat has felt more related to fasting for a spiritual purpose than to be popular or liked by others by reducing my weight. It has been an attempt to get closer to Spirit, to be seen and chosen by this force instead of be lost in the mundane insanity of typical humanness. It was not to be "seen" or admired by my fellow humans, but a way to come more deeply into contact with the source of Spirit inside and outside of myself.

It has also been about feeling very overwhelmed and confused by the feelings in my body. About experiencing how energies and emotions so intensely affect my appetite and psyche and having no clue how to deal with them. It is about my journey to try to figure all of this out—following what I thought was my hunger, my fullness, and winding up emaciated and mistrusting my own body to tell me how to nourish myself. It's about following what seemed to be my "body's wisdom" and ending up sick time and time again; the fearing of my body and mind's seeming tendency towards destruction versus nourishment. It's about learning about the Empath nature and how the energies that confuse the appetite centers, or chakras, can be guided to be helpful, not a seeming curse.

It's about starving to obtain admittance to the care of programs and structures that seem to know how to care for the body in hopes that I might learn, in hopes that my body might remember how to talk to me clearly. It's about spending time in the identity of a diagnosis, thinking there was something wrong with me, yearning for a tribe, hoping for a cure. It's about following a food plan to make sure I get "enough" to sustain my health and still ironically feeling restricted and robotic, caged and yearning for more freedom and spontaneity.

It's about fearing the trajectory of times past winding me up in a near death state. It's about my symptoms seeming to help me find a way to get out of extremely toxic environments, to get help when I had no words or connections to do so. It is about visibly portraying a message of my shadows, of the culture's shadows, when I couldn't seem to speak it. It's been about finding my voice and finding words and other ways to speak to others about my experience so I don't have to speak through starving my body or being ill. It's also about finding my way to a place of holding the tension in between the opposites, holding this idea that there is nothing wrong with me, only this journey, this experience and how I perceive and learn from it.

And it is about, of course, so many things that fan out metaphorically with food and hunger and desire and life and creativity and destruction. There is so much it is about that it is challenging for me to put it into words, but I am trying. I am trying a bit at a time, in hopes of sharing my voice, my experience, both for myself and also to those who have been struggling with these issues and have felt the typical stereotypes to be unaligned, demeaning and way off-center.

The point I mainly want to share—which hopefully came through my writing—is that there is nothing wrong with someone who is experiencing this journey called depression and/or an "eating disorder." That although diagnoses can be helpful for understanding up to a point, they more often create a sense of shame and limitation of mind within the "patient."

Imagine if this patient was actually re-framed as a seeker, called from the larger mystery to go on a journey. And that this journey is to understand, trust and learn from, and that this journey is being led from a source much larger than the Ego, from deep within the Unconscious, to craft its journeyer into a wise elder. Contemplate that if this person were to survive the journey, the point is that they would have much to offer, and that it is exactly for this reason the struggles and challenges were given to them... because there is nothing wrong with them. Contemplate that perhaps they have been pulled out from normalcy to offer the world something truly magnificent.

This is NOT to say that I think people should avoid treatment or getting help because there's "nothing wrong" with them. It is to view the need for treatment, not as a way to fix what's wrong, but rather to explore what's right. To explore why the eating disorder has come, what its teaching is, why it has pulled this particular person out of the "normal" social world (as eating disorders and depression often do in drastic ways), calling one to explore deeper layers of their personal, family, and cultural issues. It is to encourage those seeking help to see treatment as a part of the sacred process of reconnecting, re-membering parts of themselves, to see themselves as whole, and that the eating disorder may have somehow called them to undertake an initiatory journey unlike many of their peers.

This is the way I have felt called to re-frame my journey, and I aim to share it both for my own freedom of expression of my deep self, and in hopes that others may feel helped or inspired by it. This is the point.

Thank you for reading.

*A*nd in the end,
she knew
that this was just
the beginning.

RESOURCES

In case you are seeking assistance, the following books and organizations have been helpful to me on my journey.

Books

Cousineau, Phil (ed.). *The Hero's Journey: Joseph Campbell on His Life and Work.* The Collected Works of Joseph Campbell. Introduction by Phil Cousineau, foreword by Stuart L. Brown. Novato, CA: New World Library, 1998.

Duff, Kate. *The Alchemy of Illness.* New York: Pantheon Books, 1993.

Eakins, Pamela. *Tarot of The Spirit.* York Beach, MA: Samuel Weiser, 1992.

Foor, Daniel. *Ancestral Medicine: Rituals for Personal and Family Healing.* United States, Inner Traditions/Bear, 2017.

Mehl-Madrona, Lewis. *Coyote Healing. Miracles in Native Medicine.* United States, Inner Traditions/Bear, 2003.

Meredith, Jane. *Journey to the Dark Goddess: How to Return to Your Soul.* United Kingdom, John Hunt Publishing Limited, 2012.

Pinkola-Estes, Clarissa. *The Joyous Body: Myths and Stories of The Wise Woman Archetype (Dangerous Old Woman).* Narrated by Author, Sounds True, 2011. Audiobook.

Plotkin, Bill. *Soulcraft: Crossing into the Mysteries of Nature and Psyche.* United States, New World Library, 2010.

Simon, William L., and Mehl-Madrona, Lewis. *Coyote Medicine: Lessons from Native American Healing.* United States, Simon & Schuster, 2011.

Woodman, Marion. *The Pregnant Virgin.* Taiwan, Inner City Books, 1985.

------. *Addiction to Perfection.* Canada, Inner City Books, 1982.

Organizations

Carolyn Costin Institute: www.carolyn-costin.com

Ancestral Medicine: www.ancestralmedicine.org

The Marion Woodman Foundation: www.mwoodmanfoundation.org

Foundation for Shamanic Studies: www.shamanism.org

Northern Tradition Shamanism: www.northernshamanism.org

Animas Valley Institute: www.animas.org

Pacific Center: www.pamelaeakins.net

About the Author

Reagan "raVen" Lakins is a healer and Soul Guide, with a degree in Recreation Therapy and a graduate degree in Transpersonal Psychology. She offers her services through Shadowarts Healing, a vessel for providing those going through deep soul challenges with support and guidance.

raVen gained her wisdom academically and through her professional posts, including the adolescent unit at the Neuropsychiatric Insitutute of UCLA and as a Recreation Therapist and Program Coordinator at several residential eating disorder and addiction treatment centers.

Her unique attraction to the process of soul led her to leave these traditional paths of employment on adventures studying with shamanic teachers, high priestesses, herbalists, ministers and dream weavers. She has travelled the world living in intentional communities, gazing into wild seas, working on farms, and cooking in strange and magickal kitchens.

raVen currently lives on the wild coastline of Central California. Herbalism, tarot readings and dreams factor their way into her work with others, as do facilitating Rites of Passage ceremonies and Dark Goddess workshops for young women. This is her debut full-length work as a writer.

Find her cawing at shadowartshealing.wordpress.com.

Made in the USA
Columbia, SC
25 November 2020